CORNWALL'S SECRET COAST

CORNWALL'S SECRET COAST

ROBIN JONES

PiXZ

To Jenny, Vicky and Ross

First published in Great Britain in 2014
Reprinted 2016

Copyright © Robin Jones 2014
© Diamond Head 2014

*Pictures marked thus are published under
a Creative Commons licence,
the full details of which can be found at
www.creativecommons.org

British Library Cataloguing-in-Publication Data
A CIP record for this title is available from the
British Library

ISBN 978 0 85710 073 3

PiXZ Books
Halsgrove House, Ryelands Business Park,
Bagley Road, Wellington, Somerset TA21 9PZ
Tel: 01823 653777
Fax: 01823 216796
email: sales@halsgrove.com

An imprint of Halstar Ltd, part of the
Halsgrove group of companies
Information on all Halsgrove titles is
available at: www.halsgrove.com

Printed and bound in China by
Everbest Printing Investment Ltd

Front cover image: The ancient fishing village of Cadgwith where many of its thatched cottages are now second or holiday homes.

Title page image: Magnificent Porthbeor Beach lies to the south of Bonortha on the tip of the Roseland peninsula near St Mawes. CHRISTINE MOON

This page: At the foot of Cornwall's highest cliff lies the Strangles, with the rock arch known as Northern Door. JOHN WHITMARSH

CONTENTS

These giant granite boulders at Cot Valley were produced by wave action 120,000 years ago. ROBIN JONES

INTRODUCTION

Buy any standard guide to Cornwall, and it will tell you all about the perennially popular holiday resorts like Newquay, St Ives and Looe. Not this one.

If you want to visit the delectable duchy at the height of the season, but long to find a beach or cove you can have all to yourself instead of mingling with the crowds, or stunning scenery which has escaped the attention of the brochure writers, this is the book you want.

Believe it or not, Cornwall has never been completely ruined by caravan sites, souvenir shops or seaside amusements. Far from it: this book shows that there is still much of old Cornwall which lies off the beaten track: tiny fishing villages, ancient harbours, ruined mines from the duchy's industrial heydays, romantic cliff walks, and secret spots that only the locals know about.

This book is for the explorer holidaymaker: those who want to spend the morning on the beach in the time-honoured way, and in the afternoon discover something new – without having to walk the whole of the celebrated coast path.

Many of the places in this volume can be accessed by car and a short walk.

Be warned, however: many of the beaches and coves described here remain unspoiled because they are difficult to access. While all of them have footpaths leading to them, an easy but steep half-mile down to the shore has to be followed by a very strenuous return journey against the gradient.

Also, many of the beaches here are not patrolled by lifeguards because of their remoteness, and in the absence of information to the contrary, never enter the water, no matter how inviting it looks.

CHAPTER ONE

WELCOME TO CORNWALL

Everyone knows that the great River Tamar forms much of the boundary between Devon and Cornwall. The big exception, however, is in the duchy's northernmost extremity, where the honour falls to Marsland Water, a sparkling stream which races three miles westwards from Shorstone Moor, near the headwaters of the Tamar, through a wooded valley, now a Devon Wildlife Trust nature reserve to the boulder-strewn foreshore of **Marsland Mouth**.

Wade through it, or cross on the coastal path by a little foot-bridge, and you pass between the two counties. A sign marked Kernow, the Celtic name for Cornwall, marks the boundary.

The easiest way of reaching the place where Cornwall "starts" is via a bumpy dirt-track riddled with potholes which takes the motorist off a country lane at **Welcombe** and down to **Welcombe Mouth**, the last beach in North Devon.

Welcombe is an appropriate name for this place in more ways than one. It is the first village beyond Cornwall, and the

Opposite, top: Marsland Cliff towers over Marsland Mouth, where Devon ends and Cornwall begins. WILL FAICHNEY

Opposite, bottom: The jagged cliffs and Atlantic surf at Welcombe Mouth. ROBIN JONES

Below: The bridge spanning the border between Saxon England and the ancient Celtic kingdom of Cornwall. ROBIN JONES

9

magnificent spacious sands of its little-frequented beach offer a perfect haven for the sunbather, with no other facilities whatsoever.

The village includes the thatched thirteenth-century Old Smithy Inn.

Strawberry Water is typical of the Iron Coast's short streams that dash to the coast and end in a flourish, as in this waterfall at Welcombe Mouth. ROBIN JONES

The remote stretch of coastline between Hartland Point and Bude is nicknamed the 'Iron Coast' by walkers who find this unforgiving section of the South West long-distance coastal path takes far more time and more energy than any other. Lowryesque figures of walkers appear like tiny pins dotted on the tops of bleak black cliffs rising starkly to more than 400ft above the crashing waves, with the jagged teeth of eroded rock formations pointing seawards at low tide.

The sheer cliff faces are backed by a series of slender, steeply-sloping west-facing valleys or coombes, each containing tiny streams which empty themselves into the pounding surf breakers.

Each of these unspoilt valleys is well worth visiting, but there is no coastal road linking them and so they must be explored with the aid of a detailed Ordnance Survey map down steep, narrow, winding country lanes running off the "spine" route of the A39 to the east.

This is Cruel Coppinger country. Coppinger was an eighteenth-century wrecker and smuggler whose gang terrified local people for many years until revenue men ended their activities for good. But Coppinger escaped to a waiting ship and was never seen again.

From Welcombe, take the coastal path over the lofty cliff to the south and then descend to the little footbridge over the gorse-clad slate gorge gouged out by Marsland Water, or walk there from Welcombe Mouth by scrambling over the slate beds exposed at low tide.

Another way to reach Marsland Mouth is by taking a footpath along the valley, either from Gooseham Mill, now a Devon Wildlife Trust centre, which lies at the end of a very steep single-track road offering no parking at the end, or from a track off the minor road north of sixteenth-century Grade II* listed Marsland Manor, a farmhouse which is not open to the public. The track is signposted Little Marsland: park on the side before you reach a gate, and walk down. The path meets the nature trail from Gooseham Mill as it descends around 400ft over a third of a mile.

A stone memorial recalls chocolate magnate Christopher Cadbury (1908-65), who bought up pockets of land in the valley to create the nature reserve, and was also president of the Royal Society for Nature Conservation for 26 years.

Buzzards hover above the gnarled twisted oaks and dense patches of bluebells and daffodils, while more than 30 species of butterfly can be seen in the sheltered steep-sided woods in the summer.

The first coastal village in Cornwall is **Morwenstow,** a place immortalised by eighteenth-century eccentric the Reverend Robert Stephen Hawker, who ministered here from 1834-74.

He built a Gothic vicarage in the valley beneath the church, its chimneys based on the spires and towers of his favourite churches or Oxford colleges. The driftwood hut he built in

Morwenstow's parish church of St Morwenna and St John. BLADEFLYER*

11

the cliffs 150ft above the sea is the National Trust's smallest property. Hawker used to sit here to compose poetry while smoking opium.

Born in 1804 the son of a poor curate and best known for his ballad *Song of the Western Men* ("and shall Trelawny live again, or shall Trelawny die") and for reviving the Harvest Festival. Hawker married a woman older than his mother in order to complete his Oxford studies.

He dressed in seaman's boots and fisherman's garb, and occasionally wore a poncho or priestly robes like the early Celtic saints. Once he masqueraded as a mermaid and sat on a rock for several nights draped in seaweed as a joke on his bewildered parishioners.

Hawker rode a mule and toured the area with Gip, his pet Berkshire pig. He loved animals but was said to have excommunicated a cat for catching a mouse on Sunday. He died in Plymouth in 1875, and his ghost was said to have been seen on many occasions in Morwenstow.

Morwenna was, legend has it, a sixth-century Welsh saint whose chapel may have been in the small coombe known as St Morwenna's Glen.

Morwenstow's Bush Inn has been a pub since the mid thirteenth century. Previously, it was a chapel and a resting place on an ancient pilgrims' route between Spain and Wales. Inside is the wooden propeller of the De Havilland Gypsy Moth which Amy Johnson flew to Australia in 1930.

The award-winning thirteenth-century Rectory Farm & Tearoom sells refreshments.

The coastline south of Morwenstow has many stony beaches like Yeol Mouth, Cotton, Greenway and Caunter, inaccessible to the walker and viewable only from the pink sea-thrift-covered clifftops.

The next sandy stretch is at **Stanbury Mouth** and Rane beach. Park at the end of a muddy lane past Stanbury farmstead; a fifteen-minute walk down a steep but wide valley and a final scramble over rocks is the only way to the fairly sizeable low-tide beach.

The distinctive sight here is undoubtedly the gigantic white dishes of the Government Communications Headquarters (GCHQ) satellite ground station built on the former World War II airfield, RAF Cleave.

Operated by the British signals intelligence service to

Opposite: Hawker's hut: the National Trust's smallest property. ROBIN JONES

13

Already happy to lend a listening ear: the signal tracking station of GCHQ (Bude). PETER HAIR

monitor transmissions from potential threats to national security, the station, in recent times renamed GCHQ Bude, comprises 21 satellite antennas of various sizes and is surrounding by a double security fence, with every inch monitored by CCTV.

Its activities usually remain classified, but in response to concerns expressed by EU member states that GCHQ Bude was responsible for industrial espionage and the interception of civilian communications, a report by the European Parliament published in 2001 gave some details about the station.

The next worthwhile break in the rugged cliffs is **Duck-pool,** backed by Coombe Valley. A lane leading to a National Trust car park on the shore allows easy access to this shingle cove which has sand at low tide.

South of here is **Sandymouth**, easily accessible by road, with a National Trust café.

Pictured at low tide, Duckpool is isolated but can be easily reached by car.
PAUL STAINTHORP*

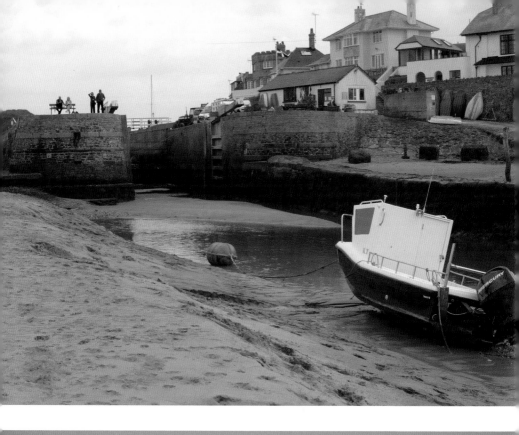

CHAPTER TWO
THE CANAL WITH TWO PORTS

B ude prospered as a resort after the arrival of the North Cornwall Railway and has long been famous for its superb stretches of golden sands and surfing waves.

However, it was an earlier form of transport which was largely responsible for creating the town. The **Bude Canal**.

Bude Haven is the name of the sandy inlet of the rocky coast through which the River Neet flows into the Atlantic. The shelly sand on the North Cornwall beaches acts as a soil conditioner and enhancer, much prized by farmers over the centuries.

Plans for a canal to carry this precious agricultural commodity to inland farms were first mooted in 1774, but it was not until 1819 that an Act of Parliament was obtained to build it.

A broad barge canal was built from Bude Haven two miles eastwards to Marhamchurch, and a tub boat canal from there to Red Post four miles away.

The line here divides into two, one stretch veering off to the north and on to Holsworthy and Thornbury, with a separate supply feeder from Virworthy and Alfardisworthy Reservoir, known today as Lower Tamar Lake.

The southern branch ran towards Launceston, in the hope of joining the navigable section of the Tamar, thereby providing a safe shipping route to eliminate the hazardous voyage around Land's End. Construction of the 35-mile Bude Canal network was completed in 1825, but the southern line finished three miles short of Launceston at Druxton Wharf.

The rails of a short narrow-gauge horse-drawn tramway, which conveyed wagons loaded with sand from Summerleaze beach to the harbour wharf to be loaded into canal boats, can still be seen set into the quayside.

The remarkable feature of the Bude Canal was its six inclined planes. The only locks on the whole length were at the harbour entrance itself and at Rodds Bridge and Whalesborough on the barge canal section. The tub boats were equipped with small wheels at the sides to allow them to be hauled on rails by chains up inclined planes – the sole

Opposite, top: The sea lock as viewed from Summerleaze Beach. ROBIN JONES

Opposite, bottom: Crowds gather to watch the reopening of Bude's sea lock in 2010 following restoration. BUDE CANAL & HARBOUR SOCIETY

The restored inland lock gate at Rodds Bridge. ROBIN JONES

way of crossing hills and valleys on the rest of the canal.
At five of the planes, Marhamchurch, Venn, Merrifield,
Tamerton and Werrington, waterwheels were used to lift up
the boats. At Hobbacott Down, which had a 1-in-4 gradient,
an ingenious bucket-in-a-well system was employed. Here,
boats were raised by filling each of two concrete buckets with
15 tons of water and allowing them to fall down 225 feet deep
wells. The water would then be released into the lower pound
and the bucket raised up again.

The Bude Canal initially cut the price of sand by about
three-quarters and increased its supply to the inland farms,
but the anticipated profits to the canal never materialised due
to high maintenance costs, and the railway killed it off after
it arrived in Bude in 1898.

Pleasure boats were introduced on the barge canal section
in 1885, and in 1891 the canal company obtained powers to
close the waterway east of Marhamchurch apart from the
Virworthy branch, which was sold to the Stratton and Bude
Urban District Council as a water supply. The canal was offi-
cially abandoned in 1912, and the two locks on the barge canal
were closed in 1924, with the drawbridges lowered into fixed
positions, preventing through navigation for anything bigger
than small rowing boats or canoes.

Apart from the pleasure boating on the harbour end, the
canal remained all but forgotten for nearly a century, despite
it being the major item of heritage interest in Bude, a resort
criticised as long ago as the nineteenth century, by the
Reverend Sabine Baring Gould as "an unpicturesque, unin-
teresting place, windblown, treeless."

Opposite, top: Lower Tamar Lake, built to supply water to the Bude Canal. SOUTH WEST WATER

Opposite, bottom: The old horse tramway which took sand from Summerleaze beach to the canal wharf. ROBIN JONES

Much of the route of the derelict and infilled canal can still be traced, and includes some public footpaths.

The Bude Canal & Harbour Society wants to improve the waterway's amenities, eventually restoring navigation for pleasure craft between the harbour and its sea lock, a unique feature on the Cornish coast, and **Helebridge Wharf**.

The wharf, which lies off the A39 town bypass, and its barge workshop have been restored and a picnic area created. Gravelled towpaths take the walker alongside two restored inland locks and from there into Bude where four new canal-side workshops have been built.

All that is now needed is for two bridges to be raised again and full-size boats will again use the whole of the barge canal between Bude and Helebridge.

Meanwhile, the separate Bude Canal Trust now owns the 5-mile Virworthy or Aqueduct branch, which ceased to be used as a public water supply in the 1980s. The trust aims to preserve the historical integrity of the largely-dry branch, which includes the system's only true aqueduct, a listed structure over the Tamar at Burmsdon, and maintain a footpath alongside. One of the old sheds at Virworthy Wharf has signboards outlining the canal's history.

A second reservoir, the 75-acre **Upper Tamar Lake**, was built north of Lower Tamar Lake in 1975. It supplies an area stretching from Crackington Haven to Clovelly.

The two lakes now offer a day out for the walker, photographer, fisherman, sailor, canoeist, cyclist and birdwatcher as well as the lost canal enthusiast. The higher reservoir has a gift shop selling local crafts and a seasonal café. Car parks for both lakes are accessed along country lanes, by following brown signs from Kilkhampton.

Yet why are we talking about an inland canal in a book about the coast?

Nine miles from the sea, across the border in Devon, lies one of the ports of the Atlantic coast – landlocked Holsworthy!

The large signs on the main roads leading into it tell us it is a 'port town' – the reason being that it once had two wharves on the Bude Canal!

Upper Tamar Lake is a modern water supply reservoir which also offers recreational facilities.

CHAPTER THREE
BENEATH CORNWALL'S HIGHEST CLIFFS

The single-track road between Widemouth Bay and Boscastle unlocks some of Cornwall's greatest geological treasures and cliffscapes.

Beware, however: reversing to let other cars pass in midsummer is no fun at all.

The little surf beach resort of **Crackington Haven** lends its name to the Crackington Formation, a geological term for the distinctive folded carboniferous sandstone and grey shale strata which underlines this part of North Cornwall and North Devon. The near-vertical cliffs beneath the coast road are renowned for their chevron-like folded sedimentary rock formations.

The shore at Crackington Haven looking north.
ROBIN JONES

Although it can be accessed by narrow road, Millook Haven is all but deserted in high summer.
ROBIN JONES

The chevron folds of the Crackington Formation exposed in Millook's cliffs.
ROBIN JONES

Stop if you can at the tiny grey pebbly beach of Millook with its scattering of houses, and you will see the twisted strata at its best. What upheavals our planet underwent over tens of millions of years to produce these effects!

Crackington, a little oasis in the cliffs, was originally a small port, although landing was an extremely hazardous venture on a coast where the jagged rocks would smash any vessel to matchwood at the first sign of high wind: this "haven" was frequently anything but.

Coastal vessels risked all to bring in limestone and coal to a kiln on the shore; slate from local quarries was taken out again. Ambitious plans to turn Crackington into a major harbour known as Port Victoria complete with a railway to Launceston received Royal Assent in 1836, but nothing came of it.

Beyond Crackington, the narrow road continues south, passing over Cornwall's highest cliff, and the steepest climb to any beach in this volume.

The path that descends to **The Strangles** is marked only by a single fingerpost off the road, from a layby opposite the entrance gate with spaces for only a handful of cars.

The twin gleaming golden sandy beaches that lie at the bottom of the path are among the most spectacular in Cornwall, yet have remained well off the well-beaten tourist track because they lie at the foot of 731ft High Cliff and a breathless climb back up.

The author Thomas Hardy visited this place in the 1870s and it inspired his novel *A Pair Of Blue Eyes*. While working as an architect on restoring the church of St Juliot near Boscastle, he fell in love with the rector's sister-in-law,

The rich veins of quartz in the slate is a distinctive feature of The Strangles.
ROBIN JONES

The expanse of the twin Strangles beaches at low tide.
ANDREW DAVIDSON

Wooden steps replace
the eroded path for
the last lap on to the
beach – with a nylon
rope to assist!
ROBIN JONES

Emma Gifford, who became his first wife.

The zig-zag path passes through huge swathes of rich purple heather and heaps of debris from cliff falls amidst the yellow gorse and bracken before the distant sands suddenly spring into view.

Wooden steps at the bottom allow access down the last few feet on to the pebbly foreshore of Strangles beach, and a nylon rope has been attached to them to provide support. The name evolved from "strange hill," as many centuries ago, a family called Strange lived hereabouts.

The combination of beach and cliffs is a piece of sheer geological wizardry, again with the strata twisted and contorted into fantastic shapes.

Here, it is easy to imagine the role of humanity as a weak

band of wretches grabbing hold of tufts of grass and the roots of plants for their very survival on a knife edge. Indeed, the imposing Samphire Rock, which divides The Strangles beach from the slightly smaller Little Strand to the north, into two, invokes the words of Edgar at the white cliffs of Dover in Shakespeare's King Lear:

"half way down,
Hangs one that gathers samphire – dreadful trade".

It is a poignant reminder of the time poor Cornish folk scraped a precarious living by gathering the dull yellow-flowering and succulent-leaved rock samphire from seemingly inaccessible nooks and crevices for pickling and sale as "crest marine", an old salad delicacy. Lose one foothold, and it was curtains.

On the far side of Little Strand beach stands Northern Door, a great wave-cut arch. A climb over the rocks towards the dragon-like headland of Cambeak leads to many caves … but watch the tide.

To the immediate south of Strangles beach is Voter Run, a jagged promontory threaded with quartz, and which is said to roar at certain states of the tide.

The Strangles beach is a Mecca for beachcombing. Fishing weights and nets, driftwood galore, containers and refuse from every nationality of vessel passing towards the Bristol Channel are washed up, and I have even found burnt-out coastguard flares.

The eerie loneliness that pervades at daybreak on Little Strand. ROBIN JONES

27

Tregardock at near low tide as seen from the clittop approach path.
FLAVIO FERRARI*

CHAPTER FOUR
SECRET SANDS BELOW THE SLATE MOUNTAIN

Again as breathtaking as the far better-known Bedruthan Steps, as remote as The Strangles, and looking every inch a cross between the two, **Tregardock beach** is another hidden jewel of the North Cornwall coast.

The nearest settlement is **Delabole**, famous for its gargantuan slate quarry, two miles away. Apart from reaching Tregardock via the coastal path, the only way there is from the farmstead at the top of a steeply-descending valley.

Turn off the B3314 at the hamlet of Westdowns and turn northwards for about two-thirds of a mile on the Treligga road. A sharp left turn down a narrow farm road leads to Tregardock Farm, where there is limited parking space.

A signposted footpath from the farm follows the middle of the valley, dotted with primroses in springtime, before its stream drops quickly towards the cliffs.

The gap in the cliffs behind the beach is dominated by the huge rocky mass known as The Mountain around which the path winds, with convenient "breathing space" ledges at the many zigzagging twists and turns. The final few yards see the extremely narrow footpath hugging the cliffside for dear life.

At low water, a huge expanse of golden sand one mile long is unveiled by the retreating breakers, as the beach joins up with Trerubies Cove, also part of the National Trust's 66 acres here, to the south.

The foreshore is marked by huge chunks of slate fallen from the cliffs and, like much of this shoreline, giant rounded boulders worn smooth over aeons by the sea. Tregardock appears to be the twin of **Trebarwith Strand** a mile and a half to the north, which, equipped with a beach café, the Fort William Inn, and a sizeable pay-and-display car park, is by comparison easily accessible. Trebarwith often gets packed at peak summer periods, but whether tempestuous or tranquil, Tregardock guarantees peace and solitude.

The cliffs are breeding grounds for many species of sea birds including fulmars, shags, razorbills and guillemots, while seals which breed undisturbed in hidden caves at the water's edge can often be glimpsed.

The stream which rises near Tregardock Farm empties itself into the sea. JENNIFER PORRETT

A surfing beach to yourself: JENNIFER PORRETT

CHAPTER FIVE

THE OTHER LUNDY

Polzeath and Daymer Bay have long been hugely-popular surfing beaches, much loved by the late Poet Laureaute Sir John Betjeman who is buried at St Enodoc's church in the dunes behind the latter.

The beaches and the sailing resort of Rock opposite Padstow frequently hit the headlines for being patronised by the celebrity set including Princes William and Harry, and Polzeath is one of the few beaches in Cornwall on which you can still park your car or VW campervan right on the sand itself.

However, a short distance away is a beach which remains truly select and secluded.

Lundy Bay, from where on very clear days you might just be able to glimpse the island of the same name, lies a mile east of New Polzeath, on an unclassified road which turns off the B3314 coastal route north of St Minver.

A public footpath from below a small National Trust car park leads down through a sheltered wooded glen leading to the 6 miles of coastal path between Pentire Point and Port Quin owned by the organisation.

In springtime, the glen is brimming with the incense and perfume of a carpet of bluebells and many species of wild-flowers dotted amongst the willow trees and blackthorn thickets, while many species of butterflies can be seen.

Reaching the coastal path, Lundy Bay lies to the east. Before you reach it there is Markham's Quay, a narrow cleft in the rocks where sand was once hauled up from the beach below for use on nearby farms.

Past there is Lundy Hole, a large natural cavity in the cliffs. The sea enters through a spectacular arch in the cliffs and waves splash over the pebbles more than 100 ft below at high tide.

This funnel-like phenomenon is a "round hole", one of several to be found in the cliffs in the Padstow locality, the most famous of all being the one at Trevone, which appears like a moon crater in an otherwise blemishless green field overlooking the sea. Such holes are the remains of collapsed sea caves, formed where waves have exploited rock fissures

Opposite, top: You have to clamber over jagged boulders to reach the sands at Lundy Bay.
ROBIN JONES

Opposite, bottom: Lundy Bay at low tide, viewed from the coast path.
ROBIN JONES

or weaker layers of strata. Eventually the cavern becomes so big that the roof falls.

Opposite: Lundy Hole, a collapsed cave. ROBIN JONES

A steep but relatively safe path leads to a useful set of steps above a foreshore covered in giant lumps of slate. As the tide recedes, a splendid firm expanse of low-tide golden sand is uncovered beyond the cliffs.

Below: The distinctive green-stone pinnacles of the Rumps behind Pentire Head. ROBIN JONES

Low tide, as well as the winding and steep cliff path, links Lundy eastwards to the smaller Epphaven Cove which is also sandy in places. A short stream cascades over the clifftops on to the rocks and boulders below.

A multitude of rockpools teem with all kinds of seashore life and enticing caves like the arch into Lundy Hole beckon the explorer. On a rockpooling expedition with the usual butterfly net I once caught a slender fish around six inches long, which we later identified as a baby conger eel.

For the energetic who fancy a longer walk, the coast path takes you eastward to the tiny harbour of **Port Quin**, while westward lies **Pentire Point** and the famous Rumps, a twin-headed greenstone promontory with an ancient hill fort reached across a narrow isthmus.

The Mouls, a craggy islet offshore, now a breeding ground for cormorants and puffins, inspired First World War poet Lawrence Binyon to write the epitaph:

"They shall not grow old, as we that are left old; Age shall not weary them, nor the years condemn."

A lazier and less time-consuming way to explore much of this coastline is aboard the pleasure cruiser *Jubilee Queen* which offers very affordable sightseeing trips from Padstow, taking you around Newland Island and The Mouls, with side-on views of the Rumps showing the ancient fort in profile.

CHAPTER SIX
THE DOOM BAR
AND THE GEYSER

Padstow's popularity soared at the end of the 1980s with the installation of lock gates on the inner harbour, allowing deepwater mooring at all times, and paving the way for a flotilla of expensive yachts to visit regularly.

The town had, however, already been the hub of a popular family beach resort for decades. Nearby St Merryn boasts of "seven bays for seven days" and the sheltered expanse of Harlyn Bay and the sandy cove of Trevone offer Atlantic breakers and surfing in relative safety.

Padstow too has magnificent beaches, but these face the Camel estuary rather than the open sea and therefore lack the big waves – and the crowds.

Follow the footpath past the war memorial to Chapel Stile and down to the little sheltered wooded inlet that is **St George's Well**, so named after a legend which tells of water gushing from a rock after being struck by a hoof of the saint's horse.

At low water you walk along the soft sand from here to **Harbour Cove**, which, backed by dunes, becomes a massive desert-like expanse. You can bathe in shallow water for several hundred yards, and sheltered from the sea breezes, it is a veritable suntrap that guarantees rapid tanning.

At Hawker's Cove on the northern side of the beach is the old Padstow lifeboat station, replaced in 1967 by a modern version at Mother Ivey's Bay.

Harbour Cove, excellent for windsurfing and kite flying, can also be accessed by a narrow road from the typically Cornish hamlet of **Crugmeer**, with a local landowner providing a car park in a sloping field, but it never becomes busy, and has no other facilities whatsoever.

Looking eastwards, the coastal path offers uninterrupted views of the treacherous submerged sandbank called the Doom Bar, the second-most dangerous stretch of English coastal waters after the Goodwin Sands off Kent.

The word actually derives from 'dune bar' – but 'Doom Bar'

Opposite, top:
The beautiful suntrap of Harbour Cove virtually deserted on a hot August day. ROBIN JONES

Opposite, bottom:
Hawker's Cove at low tide, when the Doombar becomes especially treacherous. ROBIN JONES

is certainly more apt in view of the fact that there have been around 600 wrecks there over the past two centuries alone.

Legend has it that a mermaid harpooned by a Padstow fisherman after he mistook her for a seal cursed the estuary, causing it to refill with sand again as soon as it was dredged.

In the early nineteenth century, a hollow stone rubble-built circular daymark was erected at **Stepper Point**, the 242ft headland to the west of the sandbank, as a guide to ships entering the estuary. It is now a listed building and can be visited.

The biggest wreck on the Doom Bar was the barque *Antoinette*, which became stuck on 1 January 1895 with a cargo of Welsh coal destined for Brazil. The wreck became a danger to shipping and was gelignited, the explosion reportedly shattering every window in Padstow.

The headland around the daymark has a character of its own, more akin to Dartmoor than the fields that surround Padstow.

Near the daymark is Pepper Hole, another round hole 100ft deep, and Butter Hole, an all but inaccessible sandy cove: their names may reflect commodities landed by smugglers.

The coastal path leads to the striking **Tregudda Gorge**, a favourite destination for Victorian tourists. More than 200ft deep, it is a massive black crevice in the coast with a stack rising majestically out of the murky depths.

Out to sea lies **Gulland Rock**, a small island which is now a seagull sanctuary, with Atlantic grey seals around its shores.

Top: The hollow daymark on Stepper Point. ROBIN JONES

Above: Pepper Hole, like Lundy Hole, is a 'round hole' in the cliffs west of Stepper Point. ROBIN JONES

Right: The rocky island known as Gulland Rock. ROBIN JONES

By far the best way, however, to see this coast, is not by the coast path, but from the sea. Very occasionally, the previously-mentioned *Jubilee Queen* runs an alternative to its normal trip up and down the Camel estuary, and on certain days takes passengers from Padstow out and around Gulland Rock.

A great natural geyser forms at certain states of the tide between Stepper Point and Tregudda Gorge, and it can be appreciated only from the sea.

The force of the waves funnels them through a crevice and the water repeatedly explodes in a cloud of vapour which would not look out of place in Iceland.

Beyond Tregudda Gorge are two natural archways called Porthmissen Bridge and the spectacular rock strata that is visible at the Marble Cliffs, next to the cave where the previously-mentioned Trevone round hole enters the sea.

Incidentally, an unsignposted single-track public road leads from Crugmeer to Trevone beach car park and parallels the coast path, although it does not offer the same magnificent views of the string of little coves below.

CHAPTER SEVEN:
HOLY RUINS IN CONSTANTINE'S DUNES

Constantine Bay may have been named after the first Christian Emperor of Rome, a tyrant whose subsequent conversion to the faith shaped the development of the western world.

Therefore it is ironic that this golden-sand surfer's paradise should also have been the holiday haunt of one of the world's most prominent political leaders of the twentieth century.

Constantine Bay becomes busy but never crowded in summer.
ROBIN JONES

The annual early August press conferences given by Margaret Thatcher at Trevose Golf Club became something of a tradition during her record term as Prime Minister. She stayed at a friend's holiday cottage near the end of the beach road and her burly security personnel outside always did their awkward best to look as inconspicuous as possible amongst the sunseekers.

Her presence briefly gave Constantine Bay a place on the international map, but despite its popularity as a non-commercialised version of Newquay's Fistral Bay, there is still much here to discover.

The "invasion" of the south-west peninsula by sixth-century Celtic missionaries from Ireland and Wales led to many sacred shrines springing up throughout Cornwall, often converting the name of a pagan deity or leader to that of a saint.

Sand dunes on Cornwall's west-facing shores are notorious for burying all sorts of structures and settlements, with several well-documented examples of early churches and

The setting sun throws the shadows of passers-by on to the ruins of St Constantine's chapel. ROBIN JONES

Water still seeps from the Celtic holy well of St Constantine. ROBIN JONES

holy sites lost for centuries.

Trevose Golf Club's course was laid out over an extensive dune and marshland ecosystem behind Constantine Bay. The remains of an ancient chapel and a holy well once smothered by sand are today surrounded by putting greens, but bypassed unseen by the vast majority of visitors.

Indeed, although two public footpaths cross the golf course from the road near the clubhouse northwards to Trevose Farm, both of the holy ruins are on private land.

The remains of the chapel of St Constantine stand on top of a weed-choked mound next to the nine-hole course, and below it lies a modern slate shelter which protects the ruins of the well.

The ruins are situated on what was most likely the site of a much older building, possibly dating back to the sixth century. Bishop Brantingham of Exeter ordered the structure to be reroofed in 1390 so that mass could be celebrated there three days a week. Medieval pilgrims believed the well, like most others in Cornwall, had miraculous powers, in this case to end droughts.

The little church in the dunes saw service into the early seventeenth century, when it was abandoned, probably as a direct result of the shifting sands. The locally-quarried carved Cataclews stone font from the chapel was transferred to the parish church of St Meran and St Thomas at nearby **St Merryn,** while a pier and the pinnacles of the tower were incorporated into the church at Little Petherick south of Padstow.

After it was no longer used for worship, Constantine's chapel was partitioned and turned into an almshouse for the local poor.

Despite the chapel falling into disuse, the feast of St Constantine was still celebrated on 9/10 March each year, with a hurling match taking place using a silver ball.

If this Constantine was not the emperor, who was he? Perhaps he was a son of Cornish king Cador, or the son of the sixth-century king Padarn, who fled to St David's monastery in Wales and later founded a religious settlement in Scotland.

The well building to the north of the chapel was rediscovered in 1911. Clear water still flows from the well into the stream which crosses the golf course before disappearing beneath the giant beach dunes.

To the north of the beach is **Constantine Island**, a grass-topped promontory now all but separated from the shore. An ancient settlement which once existed here has been excavated, but sea erosion has eliminated all traces of it.

Constantine Island.

Beautiful Constantine Bay as viewed from the marram grass-covered dunes immediately behind. ROBIN JONES

On the opposite side of the island lies **Booby's Bay**, at low water a northern extension of Constantine Bay, with many rockpools superb for paddling and shrimp nets.

The skeletal remains of a shipwreck exposed in the sand at certain times are those of the *Carl*, a 20,000-ton steel vessel from Hamburg impounded in South Wales at the start of the First World War and abandoned during a storm in October 1917.

The two landmark rocky islets off Constantine, the Quies, line up perfectly with Dinas Head and the Bull, the sharks-fin-shaped rock lying immediately offshore... evidence that many aeons ago the coastline was much further out than it is today, and inspiration for those who dream about the possibility of a long-lost kingdom called Lyonesse once existing between Lands End and the Scilly Isles.

Incidentally, Prime Minister David Cameron and his wife Samantha carried on the Thatcher tradition, taking summer holidays at nearby Harlyn Bay, and their youngest daughter Florence Rose Endellion, who was born in Cornwall, was given her third name after the village of the same name near Port Isaac.

Froth covering Booby's Bay the day after autumn gales. ROBIN JONES

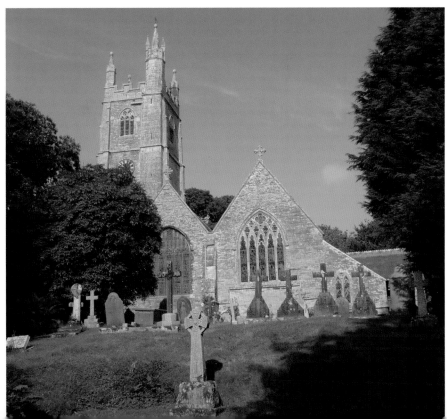

CHAPTER EIGHT

CORNWALL'S "LOVELIEST VALE"

Say it with flowers: a depiction of a Celtic cross inside the parish church porch. ROBIN JONES

That unmistakeable "clack" of leather on willow and the occasional "howzat!" interrupts the silence of a lazy summer Sunday afternoon on the village recreation ground.

Transfixed white-shirted figures of the **St Mawgan** or Vale of Lanherne village cricket teams, their opposing batsmen and umpires, are framed in green by centuries-old riverbank trees, whose branches gently sway to and fro in the whisper of a light breeze.

A swarm of gnats completes its diagonal dances in the moist air above the gurgling water as a handful of local folk watch from park benches, relaxing in the late sunshine rather than analysing the game's finer qualities.

The endless musical notes of the little river bubbling across a ford and then down its brown pebble bed into the trees is subtly mesmerising.

Standing sentinel behind its lych gate, the prominent thirteenth-century parish church oversees the sylvan scene like a watchful parent from the far side of the road.

The cooing of a wood pigeon or the whine of an occasional motor car passing through the greystone village interrupts the hazy calm. A handful of cars pull into the spaces in front

Opposite, top: The surfing beach of Mawgan Porth with its Atlantic rollers is a dramatic contrast to the peaceful sylvan village of St Mawgan 3 miles up the valley. ROBIN JONES

Opposite, bottom: The parish church of St Mauganus and St Nicholas towers above leafy St Mawgan. ROBIN JONES

The village ford in St Mawgan. ROBIN JONES

St Mawgan churchyard contains this unusual memorial to ten men who perished through cold after their ship was wrecked off Mawgan Porth in December 1846, made from wood cut into the shape of the stern of a boat. ROBIN JONES

of the village stores to deliver their occupants to the tea room behind.

An ancient bridge carries the main lane over the river and out of the village, and a few yards to the left a delightful tiny white shop beneath the sweeping boughs, sells unique gifts and local crafts. Further down the road, you are invited to inspect the dwarfish wonders of an extensive Japanese Bonsai tree nursery.

St Mawgan and the Vale of Lanherne is a place given over by both nature and man to peace and unhurried contentment...at any time of the year.

St Mawgan-in-Pydar, its full name, and its valley still manages to slumber daily through the peak season and are indeed a world apart from the busy holiday beach of Mawgan Porth where the roaring Atlantic breakers crash to the shore amidst a forest of shrieking bodyboard surfers 2 miles west. Yet both, lying on the little River Menalhyl, will always be inextricably linked with each other.

The Reverend Sabine Baring-Gould described Lanherne as "the loveliest vale in Cornwall, shut in and screened from the blasts which sweep the Atlantic."

St Mawgan was for five centuries one of the seats of the illustrious Arundell family.

In 1549, Humphrey Arundell led the famous Cornish rebellion against the Reformation and Cranmer's Book of Common Prayer. Angry at being no longer allowed to use the Cornish language for worship, 6000 men marched from Bodmin to besiege Exeter and issued their demands to London...in vain. Arundell was taken prisoner when his army was defeated and was hanged at Holborn.

The family's home in latter years, Lanherne House, above the church, was built in 1560. Since 1794 it has been occupied by a strict closed order of Teresan nuns who fled from Antwerp at the time of the French invasion and were given the house by Baron Arundell of Wardour.

St Mawgan himself was a fifth century Irish missionary who taught St David in Wales.

In spring, the marked feature of both churchyard and village is the white flower and its distinctive aroma of wild garlic.

St Mawgan's Falcon Inn is a popular place for holidaymakers to eat out in the evenings, and also for the traditional lunch before cricket matches.

A footpath from the pub runs up the valley towards Lawrys Mill and through Carmanton Woods, renowned for its rich variety of ferns. The woods contain a holy well, Nuns Well, from which a clear stream flows.

Swathes of wild garlic line the banks of the little River Menalhyl.
ROBIN JONES

The Falcon Inn lies at the heart of St Mawgan.
ROBIN JONES

Above: The
Bedruthan Steps
sands as viewed
from Pentire Steps
at the north end.
ROBIN JONES

Right: Lonely
Beacon Cove was
once used by
smugglers for landing
contraband, kegs
being stored in the
tunnels of an old tin
mine until it was
safe for them to be
hauled up and
taken away.
ROBERT SLATER

A mile north of Mawgan Porth lies the well-known beauty spot of **Bedruthan Steps**, a breathtaking series of low-tide beaches, caves, rock arches and tall stacks reached by a modern stone staircase from the superb National Trust café, based in one of the surviving outbuildings from a long-vanished nineteenth-century clifftop mine.

However, for the able-bodied, there is a lesser-known but far trickier path leading down to Bedruthan's beaches and coves, via the obscure **Pentire Steps** 2 miles further north.

To the south of Mawgan Porth lies **Beacon Cove**, sandy but unfrequented because of the very steep climb required to descend the 250ft cliffs. It can be accessed by a footpath from Trevarrian village as well as by the coast path, but is best appreciated from above.

CHAPTER NINE

THE BIGGEST WAVES OF ALL

Even the inlet known as The Gannel was insufficient to stop the post-war twentieth-century sprawl of Newquay over to Crantock and Holywell Bay, greedy to ensnare as many fine Atlantic beaches as possible with caravan villages.

However there still remains one untouched oasis where time has stood still and everything is still very much as the waves and wind rather than humans intended it to be.

Little more than a wrinkle in the cliffs on the map, Porth Joke is a rare prize that is easily worth the half-mile walk from the nearest car park.

A sheltered suntrap, this fine cove regularly boasts some of the most stupendous breakers on the whole of Cornwall's Atlantic coast.

To reach **Porth Joke**, park at West Pentire or Holywell and follow the coast path, or use a National Trust car park at Treago Mill, next to a caravan and camping park in the valley west of Cubert Common. Here, a tiny disused quarry above the entrance provides a grassy level place for a picnic.

The latter walk is on the level and therefore least demanding, especially for those carrying beach gear, and follows a gentle bramble-hedged path alongside the little valley stream running down to the golden sands.

Here are some of the biggest waves in Cornwall, a feature of the angle at which the beach faces the Atlantic. The rolling waves grow in stature until every sixth or seventh one is an 8ft to 10ft sheer wall of water. The curl of each wave poises momentarily after reaching its crescent before dreamily falling forward and smashing with full force and the very boom of thunder into a foaming torrent of white spray on the foreshore. Stand and watch for a few moments, and the effect is hypnotic.

"Joke" is believed to derive either from the Cornish "gwic", (creek) or from the word for "chough", the black crow-like bird which became a national emblem for the Cornish but which became extinct in the wild in the duchy in the 1940s.

Moves in the 1950s to desecrate Porth Joke and turn it into yet another holiday beach by allowing cars right up to the isolated foreshore thankfully came to nothing.

Opposite, main:
A long way from the dunes to the water's edge at low tide.
ANDREW CARR

Opposite, inset:
The huge Atlantic rollers funnelled into Porth Joke.
MARGIE PETERS

CHAPTER TEN
CLIFFTOP GIANTS OF INDUSTRY

Long before tourists arrived, Cornwall boasted one of the most industrialised landscapes in the world, resembling the Black Country or the South Wales coalfield at their most productive.

The duchy in the eighteenth and nineteenth centuries was for many of its inhabitants a place of unremitting graft, grind and grime, almost from the cradle to the grave.

Gigantic engine houses accomodated steam-powered beam engines which worked round the clock to pump water

The ruins of Wheal
Coates overlook the
sweep of golden
low-tide sands at
Chapel Porth.
LEE STUTT

out of tin and copper mines, some of which extended for several miles beneath the seabed itself.

Cornwall was once the world's biggest source of copper, while 150 years ago it was producing nine-tenths of European tin, but the increase in competition from Malaysia, Chile, southern Australia, Tasmania and the United States eventually sounded the death knell for Cornish mines. Heavy losses in the face of imports led to mass mine closures, causing great local hardship, and mining in Cornwall was all but dead by the Second World War.

However, Mother Nature has an uncanny way of reclaiming her own, and heavy industrial buildings which might have been considered eyesores elsewhere now enhance the romantic appeal of the Cornish landscape into which time has blended their distinctive remains.

Chapel Porth covered in snow. LEE STUTT

St Agnes (locally St Ann's) is a former port whose history is linked to its mines, the engine houses of which are still scattered around the parish. More than a hundred mines in this locality employed at least a thousand men at one stage. In the village's popular Trevaunance Cove, the ruins of a once-busy tin harbour appear at low tide.

Magical **Chapel Porth** is approached via a road from the main B3277 south of St Agnes descending 400ft through Chapel Coombe, a spectacular V-shaped gorge. At the bottom, there is a National Trust car park and a refreshments bar open during the summer months.

The moorland setting includes the remains of Charlotte United and Great Wheal Charlotte mines. A vast blanket of purple heather – sadly long since vanished from many of Cornwall's well-trodden haunts – dotted with yellow gorse now covers the old slag and spoil heaps and the foundations of the mine outbuildings, while the National Trust has taken care to keep the remains of the granite engine houses intact. Adders and lizards often bask on exposed rock.

Opposite:
The clifftop engine house at Wheal Coates.
TIM GREEN*

A cave fronted by rock pools immediately to the right of the beach opens out through the clifftop to let in sunlight and several red and green mineral-rich veins can be clearly seen.

Wheal Coates, which hangs precariously on the cliffs towards Tubby's Head to the north, and the Towanroath engine house finally closed in 1914, but left behind a much-photographed panorama for generations to admire. These buildings were restored by the Trust in 1973, and many scenes for the TV series *Poldark* were filmed here.

There is another short excursion on the northern side of St Agnes, one which is largely bypassed by most visitors.

A narrow lane from the hamlet of Trevellas on the B3285 halfway to Perranporth leads down the side of a steep valley and back up again. A short footpath leads to tiny but secluded **Trevellas Porth** and a beach of grey sand backed by pebbles.

Here are the ruins of the expansive Blue Hills tin mine which closed in 1897.

CHAPTER 11
RESKAJEAGE DOWNS AND THE NORTH CLIFFS

The B3301 coastal road between Gwithian and the old mineral harbour of Portreath appears to offer views of yellow gorse-covered Reskajeage Downs and little more. Appearances are certainly deceptive, for a few yards beyond and below the gorse lie the North Cliffs, comprising much beautiful cliff scenery and many tiny sandy coves.

The flat-topped downs are in geological terms a raised beach, formed eons ago when the sea level reached this height, but nowadays are 240ft above the waves!

Travelling east on the B3301, about a mile past the turning for Gwithian's Sandsifter bistro bar and restaurant, lies a car park. From here follow a footpath leading westwards to the sandy **Castle Giver Cove** or Smuggler's Cove, where there are the remains of a lead mine worked in the 1840s.

Next along is **Fishing Cove**, also sandy but small, where in 1870 the Tehidy Fishing Company set up its base with a small jetty and very basic quay facilities. Locals still use it to catch lobsters.

Eastwards from this car park is the famous **Hell's Mouth**, an awesome and breathtaking sheer drop.

Two caves "roar" when the breakers funnel into them, forcing out the air inside with great violence. The cliffs and the two stacks provide a safe breeding haven for tens of thousands of squawking sea birds.

Nearby Hudder Cove presents another spectacular giddy vertical, the waves which crash on the boulders below seeming as if they want to pull the onlooker down towards them.

More car parking spaces can be found above the cliff-backed **Derrick Cove** and the second of two beaches here ominously named **Deadman's Cove**, reached by an exceedingly steep path.

The finest and largest of all the beaches on this stretch is **Greenbank Cove**, where low water exposes a gleaming golden expanse of sand.

Opposite, top:
The many hidden coves and inlets beneath Reskajeage Downs. ROBIN JONES

Opposite, bottom:
The great chasm of Hell's Mouth. ROBIN JONES

Greenbank Cove
is one of the gems
waiting below the
North Cliffs. Car
parking alongside
the B3301 is readily
available.
LEE STUTT

Basset's Cove takes its name from the great landowners whose estate comprised much of this district until the First World War.

The family may have come to England with William the Conqueror and acquired the manor of Tehidy to the south of Reskajeage Downs through marriage in the twelfth century.

They used Portreath and the North Downs for recreational purposes when in residence at their mansion at Tehidy; Spratting Cove was renamed Basset's Cove (the old name for Portreath) during the 1880s and a summerhouse was built there.

Basset's Cove and the nearby car parks are linked by a series of footpaths to 250 acres of woodland sheltered behind the downs, providing a direct contrast to the bracing clifftops.

The V-shaped Carvannel Valley provides a surprise and sheltered variation in otherwise flat terrain, opening out into **Porthcadjack Cove**.

Just off the coast is Samphire Island, another place where impoverished locals once risked all to gather the ancient delicacy described in Chapter 3. Many hidden rocky inlets only visible from boats are now left to the grey seals who breed here.

The shadowy rocky fissure of Ralph's Cupboard is said to be named after a giant, Wrath, who lived in a cave where he ate hapless fishermen and sailors, after wading out to sea to grab their ships. When he died, the roof of his home collapsed, leaving the gorge we have today. A more plausible story relates how a smuggler called Ralph once stored his contraband here.

Spacious sandy **Western Cove** is hidden by Western Hill from **Portreath**, now a small but popular modern holiday and surfing resort.

The Tehidy estate in what is broadly its present form was developed by the Bassets in the mid-eighteenth century when the family built a new large mansion here on the site of their historic seat. Cornwall County Council bought most of the surviving landscaped parkland in 1983 and turned it into a vast public country park, offering more than 9 miles of footpaths through woods and alongside streams.

The old mining port of Portreath has seen much new tourist-based development in recent years. ROBIN JONES

Portheras Cove is
well worth the
half-mile walk from
Pendeen lighthouse.
LEE STUTT

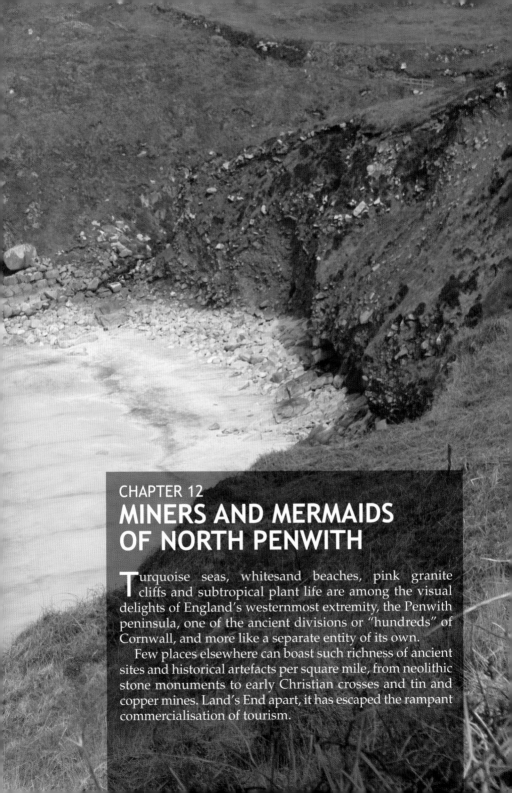

CHAPTER 12
MINERS AND MERMAIDS
OF NORTH PENWITH

Turquoise seas, whitesand beaches, pink granite
cliffs and subtropical plant life are among the visual
delights of England's westernmost extremity, the Penwith
peninsula, one of the ancient divisions or "hundreds" of
Cornwall, and more like a separate entity of its own.

Few places elsewhere can boast such richness of ancient
sites and historical artefacts per square mile, from neolithic
stone monuments to early Christian crosses and tin and
copper mines. Land's End apart, it has escaped the rampant
commercialisation of tourism.

The B3306 which runs westwards from St Ives to St Just is quite unlike any other road in the south west; the landscape it passes has much more in keeping with the Western Highlands of Scotland. Twisting and turning around ancient farmsteads and ruined barns, past the ghostly relics of deserted engine houses, across purple heathland and skirting tor-topped hills, it reduces to single track in places.

A marked feature is the patchwork patterns of drystone-walled fields which date back to the Bronze Age.

The coastline, well concealed from the road, could easily be Hebridean by virtue of its towering cliffs, rocky pinnacles and many secret inlets; yet equally its exquisite beaches and hidden coves might be described as Mediterranean.

An easy starting point for exploration is the tiny granite moorland village of **Zennor**, with its delightful Wayside Museum and church of St Senara.

The little folk museum houses a collection of farming, fishing, mining and domestic implements, a blacksmith's forge and a nineteenth-century laundry, and an iron water-wheel turns outside.

The Tinners Arms was built in 1271 to accommodate masons working on the village church opposite. Zennor and its church are famous for the tale of the mermaid and the squire's son Matthew Trewhella, with whom she fell in love after hearing him singing in the church and lured him into the sea; never to be seen again.

Below the tower is a memorial to John Davey, 1812-91, said to be the last person in the parish to know the Cornish, more than a century after Mousehole's much-vaunted Dolly Pentreath, popularly held to be the last speaker of the language.

A level path leads through the farm on the left and north-wards for half a mile to Zennor Head, 300ft above sea level, and resplendent in its covering of yellow gorse, purple ling and bell heather.

The granite and killas cliff drops off suddenly below the path to reveal two V-shaped coves of creamy sand with waves from a translucent blue-green sea almost straight off an artist's mixing palette gently lapping their fringes, stunning in their beauty.

A steep footpath down the valley of the village stream accesses the nearest, **Pendour Cove**, where the mermaid and her lover disappeared beneath the waves; it is said their

The twin beach of Pendour Cove and Veor Cove fronted by a turquoise sea.
ROBIN JONES

singing can often be heard.The other beach, **Veor Cove**, backed by unyielding cliffs, is accessible only by a scramble over the low water rocks from the first.

The coast path runs eastwards past the remains of several old mine workings to the National Trust's Tregethen Cliffs and the inlet of Wicca Pool 2 miles away. *Lady Chatterley's Lover* author D H Lawrence and his German wife Frieda lived in a cottage near here from 1915-17 while he wrote *Women In Love*; wild rumours that they were enemy spies who signalled to submarines from the clifftops were not helped by the fact her cousin was Mannfred von Richtofen, the Red Baron air ace. The couple were accordingly driven out of Zennor.

The path winds past Economy Cove and then the twin islets known as the Carracks come into view. Seals bask here, and boat trips are run from St Ives to see them.

A circular walk back to Zennor follows the steep valley up from stony River Cove to Trevail Mill and on to Boscubben, Wicca, Tregethen and Tremedda farms.

At Zennor stands the Giant's Rock, a quarter of a mile north of the church. This 22ft long boulder rests on top of another massive stone, and natural hollows in the top resemble armchairs.

The imposing greenstone promontory of **Gurnards Head**, named after its resemblance to the fish, is reached by a two-thirds of a mile walk from the hamlet of Treen, a mile west of

Zennor, turning off at the Gurnards Head Inn.

Treen Cove, a sandy cove which nestles below Gurnards Head to the east, is a lonely and unpopulated spot today. On the neck of the headland stand the remains of twelfth-century Chapel Jane, including a stone bench and altar slab.

The coast path westwards hugs the 300ft contour for a while before descending to **Porthmeor Cove**, a shingly scallop-shaped inlet with patches of low-tide sand again encompassed by awesome cliffs. A shorter walk down a valley leading here from the main road may be undertaken from near Lower Porthmeor Farm.

The B3306 turns under the shadow of the boulder-strewn twin peaks of Carn Galver and Watch Croft, at 827ft the highest point on the Penwith peninsula and past the disused Carn Galver Mine buildings half a mile west of Lower Porthmeor.

The mine's count house is now used by the Climbers Club of Great Britain, whose members revel in the many vertical drops on this coast, especially at nearby Bosigran Cliff, famous for its 650ft Commando Ridge climb, nicknamed after the Marine Commando Assault Wing which trained there during World War Two in preparation for wartime cliff assaults. In 1963, Lord Hunt and Sherpa Tensing climbed here

Alongside the B3306 stands Carn Galver Mine, where the giant beam engines stopped pumping in 1871. ROBIN JONES

to celebrate the tenth anniversary of the conquest of Everest.

A short descent down the once heavily-industrialised Porthmoina valley leads to a little cove. The fast-flowing valley stream, aided by a series of reservoirs, powered a series of tin stamps and one example, Porthmoina Mill, can be seen near the coast path.

A mile-long walk from **Porthmoina Cove** takes you past Whirl Pool and over the equally impressive Trevean and Morvah Cliffs, from where a path leads south to lonely Morvah village and its restored fifteenth-century church, back on the B3306.

The utterly magnificent **Portheras Cove** is the most accessible of all the little sandy beaches on the north coast. It can be reached either by a farm track (difficult parking) or a mile-long field path from **Morvah**, or more conveniently, by driving to **Pendeen lighthouse** 2½ miles by road.

From the lighthouse, take the coast path eastwards for about half a mile. The path slopes down over Pendeen and Portheras Cliff to a large expanse of golden-white sand exposed at low tide, interspersed with the giant sea-smoothed granite boulders typical of the Penwith coast.

Pendeen lighthouse was built in 1900 when the top of the headland was flattened. It was automated in 1995. ROBIN JONES

CHAPTER 13
CAPE CORNWALL:
THE ORIGINAL LAND'S END

St Just-in-Penwith could easily capitalise on its position as "last town in England" to follow in the wake of "first and last house", "last pub", "last stones" and the like at Land's End 6 miles to the south, but it is to the granite former mining town's great credit that it has not embraced mass commercialisation.

Similarly, the coastline around St Just, named after a sixth-century Breton missionary, has avoided the blemish of mass commercialisation, despite the fact the promontory of Cape Cornwall was once considered far more of a landmark than Land's End.

Having the in-Penwith tag to distinguish it from St Just-in-Roseland, it was the heart of a thriving mining, farming and fishing community. Now it is a quiet unruffled place apart from market days and its annual Feast Day.

A mile to the west lies the 229ft-high humpbacked promontory of **Cape Cornwall**. The lack of 1,000 yards has led to it remaining unspoiled. Had it managed that extra distance, it would be famous as England's westernmost point instead of Land's End having the title.

Seafarers traditionally considered Cape Cornwall the more important of the two because it was the dividing line between the English Channel and St George's Channel on their charts. Herein lies the reason why it is England's only "cape", a term referring to the place where two oceans meet.

Mined from the start of the Seventeenth century, Cape Cornwall is riddled with old shafts. The stack on its summit was once part of Cape Cornwall's mine, worked from 1836-79 with tunnels which ran out under the sea as far as the Brisons or Sisters, the dreaded twin rocks where many ships have been wrecked over the centuries, including the brig *New Commercial* in 1851 with the loss of nine lives. Miners often said they could hear the Atlantic breakers crashing on the rocks above their heads!

The Heinz company of 57 varieties fame bought the cape for the National Trust in 1987 from the Oats family, whose ancestor Francis Oats made his fortune after emigrating to South Africa

Opposite, top:
Cape Cornwall,
England's only cape.
SHIROKAZAN*

Opposite, bottom:
St Just town centre
contains traditional
old inns and old-fash-
ioned shops run by
the same families for
many generations.
The old market house
is now the Wellington
Hotel on the left.
ROBIN JONES

Below: The landmark
chimney stack of
Cape Cornwall Mine.
ROBIN JONES

71

The Brisons as viewed from Cot Cove. JIM CHAMPION*

and later returned to build Portledden House, landscaping the scarred headland with many trees and shrubs.

Under the southern wing of Cape Cornwall is **Priest's Cove**, a tiny low-tide shingle beach. A car park is available and a swimming pool for children has been created in the rocks. The ruins of a building named as St Helen's chapel stand in a field on the neck of the cape.

Priest's Cove has a slipway and an assortment of small brightly-painted boats and wooden fishermen's stores used for crab and lobster fishing. ROBIN JONES

South of Priest's Cove is Carn Gloose, where Ballowall Barrow, the largest Bronze Age burial mound in Penwith, can be inspected. It also can be reached by car from the first turning left off the Cape Cornwall road outside St Just.

The next place southwards on the coast path is **Cot Valley**, which on a bright, clear sunny day is somewhere very special indeed. Going by car, take the Cape Cornwall road from the town square but turn left before the primary school, and follow Bosorne Road past a housing estate. The road descends to the cluster of cottages at Bosorne and then winds its way down into the little valley. It is well worth the trip.

The single-track road abruptly ends above the shore, where there are a handful of free parking spaces, but no facilities.

Low tide at **Porthnanven** or Cot Cove reveals a beach between the lofty cliffs covered in rounded white and beige granite boulders, looking every bit like giant speckled dinosaur eggs! Clamber over them and you step on to a patch of charcoal-grey sand through which the little stream rushes to join the Atlantic.

The similar **Nanquidno Valley** is accessed via the first turning right off the B3306 south from St Just immediately before you reach Land's End Aerodrome. The roadway ends at Nanjulian Farm from where a steep 500-yard walk leads to Maen Dower and the shore below the National Trust's Bodregan holding.

A clamber northwards over the boulders at low tide leads to Polpry Cove, the 'clay pool', which has many caves.

A native of South Africa, the Hottentot Fig grows around Cape Cornwall and elsewhere in Cornwall.
ROBIN JONES

The distinctive boulders of Porth Nanven or Cot Cove.
ROBIN JONES

CHAPTER 14
UNTYPICALLY TROPICAL

The southern coast of Penwith sharply contrasts with the northern and western sides of the peninsula.

Making the most of the Gulf Stream, the sheltered valleys sprout rare and exotic plant life in abundance.

Rather than grim inhospitable jagged cliffs with the occasional begrudged cove or crevice, there is a plethora of idyllic little sandy beaches and tiny fishing harbours, each a work of art in itself.

Working eastwards, **Nanjizal** or **Mill Bay**, 2 miles south of Land's End, has lost much of its sand through winter storms but none of its charm.

Nanjizal is approached by stopping at the hamlet of Polgigga on the B3315 between Lands End and Newlyn. A footpath runs along a private trackway to Higher Bosistow Farm, which can alternatively be reached by a route marked "road used as public path" on the Ordnance Survey map from the Porthgwarra road – but check your exhaust pipe first if you decide to risk your car!

Cliffs composed of pillars of fractured granite soar on either side of the boulder-strewn cove, and a waterfall cascades through a spectacular vertical arch on the left-hand

Opposite: The Song of the Sea arch at Nanjizal.
MASA SAKANO*

Nanjizal or Mill Bay lies beneath Lower Bostitow Cliff.
LEE STUTT

The harbour at
Porthgwarra
comprises this tiny
slipway. ROBIN JONES

side. Seals can occasionally be glimpsed.

The coast path between here and Porthgwarra has many rocky inlets including Pendower Cove, Zawn Kellys, Folly Cove and Porth Loe. The promontory of Gwennap Head and Tol-Pedn-Penwith, the "holed headland in Penwith", so called because of a funnel-shaped chasm created by the collapse of a sea cave, is the western limit of Mounts Bay.

Gwennap Head, nicknamed "the fisherman's Land's End", is where the English Channel and St George's Channel physically meet: Cape Cornwall was only the estimated point on old navigational charts.

Tiny **Porthgwarra** may have been founded by fishermen from Brittany. Its picturesque little cottages are reached by a winding 2-mile long road also off the B3315 at Polgigga, or by a ten-minute walk from Gwennap Head.

Lobster fishing is still carried on from a cove above a tiny sandy beach backed by seaweed-covered boulders. Two short tunnels were cut by St Just miners, one to allow farmers to collect sand as fertiliser and the other allowing fishermen to access shellfish stores in the rocks prior to taking their catches to market.

Half a mile further eastwards on the coast path, **St Levan Churchtown** is reached. There is also a car park behind the thirteenth-century parish church. From here, a signposted footpath leads down a short valley to the enchanting low-tide beach of **Porth Chapel**.

Take a glance at **Porthcurno** from the coast path on a sunny day, and then say that what lies below is not the most beautiful beach you have viewed anywhere.

The white sand underlying the waves creates the distinctive turquoise colour typical of Penwith beaches. At exceptionally low tides the sloping beach joins up with other coves in the startlingly spectacular pink and golden-brown granite bay between Minack Point and Treryn Dinas headland to form a continuous chain.

Pedn-Vounder beach, an unofficial naturist beach, is backed by the stunning granite cliffs of Treryn Dinas. The headland to the east of the beach is the location of the famous Logan Rock, a rectangular block of granite which weighs about 70 tons, and which can be rocked back and forth by one person. In 1824, young naval lieutenant, Hugh Colvill Goldsmith, nephew of the writer Oliver Goldsmith, and his crew toppled it as a joke, but he was forced to re-erect it at his own expense. It and the Logan Rock Inn in unspoilt Treen village to the north are owned by the National Trust.

An exotic beach above a maze of tunnels and cables communicating with the rest of the world. James Bond? No – Porthcurno! ROBIN JONES

The rocking Logan rock at Treen. JIM CHAMPION*

A 2007 production of
The Tempest at the
Minack Theatre.
ROBIN JONES

Clinging to the cliffside to the immediate west of Porthcurno is the unique **Minack** open-air theatre. Land-owner Rowena Cade was so enraptured by the open-air performance of *A Midsummer Night's Dream* in a wooded setting at St Buryan three miles away in 1929 that she decided to carve her own theatre out of the cliffs 200ft above sea level. Assisted by her gardener and a friend, a basic stage and auditorium was ready summer 1932 for its first production, Shakespeare's *The Tempest*.

She died in March 1983, by which time the once-unforgiving cliffside had become not only a unique 750-seater auditorium but a major tourist attraction, with a 16-week summer season and a separate exhibition centre telling its story. What other stage can boast such a backdrop?

Many summer visitors to Porthcurno may not be aware that lying several feet beneath their beach towels was the start of a major worldwide communications network, the 'Victorian internet'.

Porthcurno, "Port of Cornwall", was chosen as the British terminus for the world's first underwater telegraph cable, laid across the Atlantic in 1866.

In 1890, the final link in a chain connecting London to Gibralter, Malta, Suez and Bombay was completed.

By the 1930s, all telegraph communications to and from the British Empire passed below the beach, cables linking Britain

EASTERN TELEGRAPH COMPANY

to the United States, western Canada, South Africa, China and Hong Kong...a phenomenal 155,000-mile network.

The telegraph relay station in the Porthcurno valley was moved into tunnels blasted into the cliff sides during the second world war to protect it from Luftwaffe air attacks. Its unique underground secrets are now displayed in the splendid Porthcurno Telegraph Museum for all to marvel at.

Few places encapsulate the spirit of south Cornwall as the little fishing cove of **Penberth**, an absolute gem. Its stone fishermen's cottages above a little slipway, with about a dozen small fishing boats beached above the shoreline suggest a perfect harmony between man and nature, a Cornish garden of Eden. Exotic flowering plants grow to amazing heights in the natural warmth of the valley's microclimate.

From here to Mousehole, the coast is dotted with parcels of land divided into 'quillets', small meadows where daffodils, violets and potatoes were grown in abundance for early markets because of the early high temperatures.

The flora is even more tropical in appearance by the time

Original cable transmission equipment deep inside the telegraph museum. ROBIN JONES

79

St Loy's Cove
surrounded by lush
vegetation. ROGER
BUTTERFIELD

the lonely scattered houses of **St Loy** are reached nearly 2 miles to the east along the coast path.

The long boulder-covered beach exposed at low water forms part of the coast path and alternatively can be reached by a very pleasant half-mile walk along a wooded valley from Trevedran Farm.

Beyond Boscaven Point can be seen Tater Du lighthouse, which dates from 1965, and beyond it the 20-acre flower farm where author Derek Tangye, famous for his cat-themed novels, lived with his wife Jeannie.

The well-known little granite harbour of **Lamorna Cove**, accessed by a steep road from Lamorna village, was built in 1854. The flower-strewn woodland and trout stream in the valley behind it have long attracted artists from the famous Newlyn School.

Owned by the National Trust since 1957, fishing still continues at Penberth, where the tiny harbour and beach never get crowded.
ROBIN JONES

CHAPTER 15
SOMETHING STIRRING IN THE VAULTS

A s an image in every guidebook to Cornwall and clearly visible for many miles around, **St Michael's Mount** with its medieval castle is the last place you might expect to be featured in a book about obscure places on the coast.

However, every great fairytale castle absolutely must have a secret, and this one is no exception. While Cornwall is a great land of dubious myths and legends, this one is for real, and yet very few of the 200,000 annual visitors stumble across it.

Above: Fairytale setting: St Michael's Mount at high water, when the causeway linking it to Marazion is covered by the sea. ROBIN JONES

Opposite: The railway's sole item of rolling stock delivers a cargo of old newspapers to the quayside station. ROBIN JONES

Deep within the granite rock on which the castle sits runs its own railway, one which has operated almost every day since it was built in 1901. It is not a model, a seaside miniature pleasure line, a toy or a gimmick, but a real working freight-carrying line.

The unique 2ft 5in gauge cable-operated incline line runs from a bottom station next to the island's harbourside, from where supplies for the castle are loaded into a wagon, to a

The short length of
2ft 5in gauge railway
set in the island quay
is the only part of
the line that the
public see.
ROBIN JONES

summit station in the castle's kitchen pantry.

The line is around an eighth of a mile long, and has a slope of 1-in-1.9 as it climbs 174ft between the quay and the pantry.

The National Trust, which administers the island, does not allow public access to the railway. For visitors, the only clue to its existence is the short length of rail laid tramway-style on the quayside beyond a set of wooden double doors between the harbourside cottages that lead to its base station, known as the `tramyard'.

Apart from one section where tunnelling through the granite was essential, the railway was built by Cornish miners on the `cut-and-cover' principle with a brick arch to conceal it from view.

The railway, which replaced the packhorses that once hauled provisions up the hill, has a single item of rolling stock – a steel wagon which is hauled up and down the line by a cable connected to an electric-operated winding drum at the summit station.

This railway never saw steam traction. Power was originally supplied by a gas engine, but a Ruston petrol engine replaced it in the 1920s. When an 11,000-volt power cable supplying the island from the mainland was installed in 1951, the engine was replaced by a motor.

Prior to an upgrade in 1988 to meet modern safety standards, there had been several accidents on the railway, some which led to the wagon overshooting the buffer stops, smashing through the quayside wall ... and ending up in the sea.

Luckily, there were never any injuries. In earlier days, the railway ran at speeds of up to 40mph, but since the modifications were made, the train now takes a more modest 2mins 35secs to cover the entire trip at a more controlled speed. Before World War Two, the possibility of converting the line for passenger use was briefly considered: in past times seasonal staff had a tradition of riding inside the wagon as a rule-breaking dare at least once during their six-month summer spell.

Below left: The tunnel inside the hill was dug by Cornish miners. ROBIN JONES

Below right: The winding gear at the summit. ROBIN JONES

CHAPTER 16

A CASTLE OF ILL REPUTE AND THE KING OF SMUGGLERS

L ooking every bit a typical square village church tower rather than a fortified manor boasting a long, illustrious and notorious history, it is little wonder that the remains of **Pengersick Castle** are as often as not passed by without a second glance.

The Grade I* listed Tudor castle, a Scheduled Ancient Monument, is now in the care of the Pengersick Historic & Education Trust, established by late owner Angela Evans, who lived in it for thirty-five years and died in late 2008.

Privately maintained, Pengersick has escaped the attention of the glossy tourist attraction brochure writers. Despite its location in the centre of the popular holiday village of Praa Sands, and easily spotted from the main A394 between Marazion and Helston, it was opened only by prior appointment.

Opposite: Pengersick Castle, home to one of Cornwall's most infamous families. PENGERSICK HISTORIC & EDUCATION TRUST

Below: Lawless Pengersick Castle in the days of yore.

To the east of Prussia Cove, beautiful Kenneggy beach is a much larger expanse of excellent sand to be enjoyed. Kenneggy is reached only by a scramble over rocks at low tide as the cliffs which back it are far too steep to climb.
YVETTE ANSELL*

Henry Pengersick or Le Fort was lord of the manor in 1330. He was first blamed for the legend of the notorious Pengersicks, being excommunicated for wounding Daniel Lyspein, the vicar of nearby Breage who was gathering tithes, but received absolution from the Pope five years later.

The inheritance passed to Isabella Worth in 1442 and her husband Thomas may have rebuilt the original castle, turning it into a fortified dwelling with twin towers.

John Milliton of Meavy near Dartmoor, who married the

Worth heiress Elizabeth, was accused of plundering treasure from a Portuguese shipwreck at Gunwalloe in 1526. Milliton and two other prominent landowners, including William Godolphin, were later acquitted following a lawsuit brought by the Portuguese government, which nearly declared war with England over the issue. Milliton went on to become a justice of the peace, governor of St Michael's Mount and High Sheriff of Cornwall.

A tale recounts that Milliton's son William and his wife Honor successfully contrived to poison each other at dinner, but others say she lived for more than 30 years after him.

Because William's male heir, also William, had been lost at sea in 1571 shortly before his father died, the property was split between six daughters, none of who had sufficient income to maintain the castle, which fell into decay.

The surviving tower was obviously designed for defensive purposes. Commanding superb views over Mounts Bay, gave early warning of approaching hostile ships. The defeat of the

Another exquisite beach, this time on the opposite side of Praa, is Porthcew below Rinsey Head, reached by a steep track also cut by smugglers. The ruins of the Wheal Prosper tin and copper mine engine house and stack on the headland are owned by the National Trust. LEE STUTT

Spanish Armada did not end that country's threat to Britain; only seven years later in 1595, the Spaniards raided and burned Mousehole, Penzance and Marazion. A "drop slot" for pouring boiling oil over the heads of an attacking force from above the doorway is still evident.

John Carter, the "King of Prussia" who also held sway in these parts, could never boast of aristocratic connections like the Pengersicks, but was no less colourful.

A swashbuckling eighteenth-century smuggler who showed scant regard for authority, Carter was locally a popular figure who even ran an inn. From 1777 until 1807, he conducted a non-stop game of cat-and-mouse with the excisemen and in 1783 even mounted his own battery of guns on the cliffs near Cudden Point, using them to fire on a Revenue cutter.

One day Carter's entire load of French contraband was seized by the preventive men – only for him to mount a counter attack and recover it all from the custom house store in Penzance the same night...without taking an additional single item! Truly a prince amongst rogues!

Carter's nickname now lends itself to **Prussia Cove**, a jagged pebbly inlet used as a harbour by tiny fishing boats previously known as Porthleah.

Dusk at Prussia Cove in early May.
ROBIN JONES

Safe haven in a classic smuggler's cove! A small rowing boat berthed in a natural rocky inlet at Prussia Cove.
ANDY DUNSTAN

A lane from Rosudgeon on the A394 takes you to a car park about ten minutes on foot from this beach. Alternatively, the coastal path reaches the cove a mile west from Praa Sands. Either way, it is a steep haul back up from the shore.

To the right of Prussia Cove is the chasm of Pixies Cove and its caves, noted for spectacular wave action during rough seas. On the opposite side is Bessie's Cove, the site of a smugglers' inn owned by Carter's associate Bessie Burrows.

Old fishermen's sheds at Prussia Cove.
MARI BUCKLEY*

CHAPTER 17
STILL WATERS ABOVE
A RAGING SEA

"...all day long the noise of the battle roll'd,
Among the mountains by the winter sea,
Until King Arthur's Table, man by man,
Had fallen in Lyonesse about their lord,
King Arthur. Then, because his wound was deep,
The bold Sir Bedivere uplifted him,
And bore him to a chapel nigh the field,
A broken chancel with a broken cross,
That stood on a dark strait of barren land;
On one side lay the Ocean, and on one
Lay a great water, and the moon was full."

Tennyson, The Passing Of Arthur

It has been claimed that Alfred, Lord Tennyson's scene of Sir Bedivere's reluctant surrender of the sword Excalibur to the Lady of the Lake and the death of Arthur was set at **Loe Pool** near Helston.

The freshwater lake was formed by a natural bar dividing the sea from freshwater built up behind it and which permeates through the sand and shingle to escape.

However, while Arthur is generally held to have been a fifth century Romano-British leader, Loe Pool did not exist until the twelfth century, when the massive sandbar was formed by coastal drift, cutting off the estuary of the little River Cober, on which the nearby town of Helston had developed as a port, and leaving it high and dry.

Loe Pool is a place of isolation and solitude which has a markedly eerie feel, especially in the fading light after dusk. Hemmed in by gentle rolling hills, it has a dark, still, brooding, even menacing and unworldly atmosphere at times, as if the still silent waters are trying to lure you into them.

You cannot drive to Loe Pool or Bar by public road; you must walk there. Car parks are sited at Helston itself, Penrose near Porthleven, Highburrow near the Tye Rock Hotel overlooking

Opposite, top:
A creek of Loe Pool.
TIM GREEN*

Opposite, bottom:
Not even a ripple
on Loe Pool.
TIM GREEN*

Porthleven Sands, and Chyvarloe on the Gunwalloe side of Higher Pentire, about a mile south-west of RAF Culdrose. A walk around the whole perimeter of the pool is about 5 miles.

Starting at Helston, park opposite the town's recreation ground and Coronation boating lake, which may well have been the site of the ancient harbour. Paths lead down on either side of the Cober to a newly-installed causeway and bridge; this allows a circular walk of the pool to be undertaken.

Beyond here is Loe Marsh, where the old estuary became silted up largely due to the alluvial deposits brought down by the Cober from its tin mining hinterland. A silver and lead mine, Castle Wary, or Wheal Pool, was sited here, and the plans for an offbeat and highly-ambitious eighteenth-century project using an innovative wind-powered dredger (which was never built) to reclaim valuable minerals from the silt are preserved on display in Helston's museum.

Loe Pool is just over a mile in length from the edge of the marsh to the sandbar, and is about 10ft above sea level and 30ft deep.

The less muddy path, that on the western side of the lake, follows several drives and walkways and was built to serve the surrounding Penrose estate, leading through an oak coppice and into the estate grounds.

Palm trees and a bamboo grove grow here. The 1554-acre estate including Loe Pool, were given by the Rogers family to the National Trust in the 1970s, on condition that the tranquility of the lake and surrounding land was to be preserved forever. The seventeenth-century manor house is not open to the public.

The path continues from Penrose for a mile through Bar Walk Plantation, hugging the side of the lake, where four old boating jetties can be seen. It emerges on to the shore at Bar Lodge, and only then can the strangeness of the natural barrier separating lake from sea be fully appreciated.

The winding eastern walkway passes through Deginba Wood and around the lake's own 'inlet', Carminowe Creek, where it is joined by paths from Higher Pentire and Chyvarloe car parks.

A shady shore of Loe Pool.
JASON CARTWRIGHT*

CHAPTER 18
THE OLD SERPENTINE FACTORY

The souvenir shops at Lizard Town, Britain's southernmost village, thrive on a single commodity – carved ornaments made from grey-green serpentine rock.

The southern tip of the plateau-like Lizard peninsula, is comprised of this beautiful rock, which manifests itself in shades of red, green, yellow, black and cream, as seen in the spectacular jagged cliffs at Kennack Sands, Lizard Point and, of course, the popular tourist magnet of Kynance Cove. Often greasy to the touch, some chunks are little heavier than a correspondingly-sized piece of lava or pumice.

The softness of serpentine which allows it to be easily carved, turned, shaped and polished to a mirror-like finish

Poltesco serpentine works in its nineteenth-century heyday. ILLUSTRATED LONDON NEWS

have formed the basis of a thriving industry around the Lizard for the past two centuries.

The visit of Queen Victoria to Penzance in 1846 turned the serpentine cottage industry into a national concern overnight. She bought several serpentine ornaments, and suddenly everyone had to have their own pieces too.

After examples of serpentine craftsmanship featured in the Great Exhibition of 1851 at the Crystal Palace, demand led to serpentine workshops mushrooming around the Lizard.

Turned lighthouses a speciality: a nineteenth-century serpentine craftsman at work. ROBIN JONES COLLECTION

The ghostly ruins
of Poltesco's once-
prosperous
serpentine works
at Caerleon Cove.
MARTIN BODMAN*

The biggest factory was set up in the hamlet of Poltesco in 1866, in old pilchard cellars above pebbly **Caerleon Cove**.

The factory's prosperity soared, and soon a quay was built alongside in the mouth of the stream which gurgles down the enchanting Poltesco valley. From here, barges took out the finished products to cargo ships moored offshore which took them to London or exported them to the continent.

Vases, tables, fireplaces and even shop fronts were manufac-

Little Cove,
with Caerleon
Cove behind.
GRAEME DALEY

tured. A 25ft diameter waterwheel provided the power to turn the machinery and a stationary steam engine was later added.

The works employed 23 hands in 1883, but fashions changed, and the business was finished by 1893. Cheap marble imports was one major factor blamed for this.

One tale has it that the factory received a huge order for fireplaces for a chateau in France. An uninsured barge transporting the finished goods was lost at sea, and the losses were too great for the little factory to bear.

The empty three-storey factory was eventually abandoned. The site is now owned by the National Trust.

A circular walk down the delightful sheltered Poltesco valley to the cove can take no more than twenty minutes. Off the single-track signposted road from Ruan Minor lies a small National Trust car park in Poltesco Farm yard.

Those with longer to spare may fancy the mile-long walk southwards over the cliffs to the picture-postcard fishing village of **Cadgwith**, a 'must paint' destination for generations of artists, with its serpentine cottages, some of which have thatched roofs chained to them to resist storms.

The ancient fishing village of Cadgwith where many of its thatched cottages are now second or holiday homes.

CHAPTER 19
THE QUARRIED COAST

While the ruins of the great engine houses of tin and copper mines have, bizarrely, enhanced the romance of the Cornish landscape, on parts of the eastern side of the Lizard peninsula, mineral extraction has disfigured the coast.

Gigantic quarries both disused and still being worked now dominate stretches of what were once cliffs between Coverack to the south and Porthallow to the north.

However, quarries are an essential source of building materials, and if the Not In My Back Yard fraternity had their way, in theory we could be left with nothing from which to build houses and roads.

Gabbro, otherwise known as "black granite", was extracted from **Dean Quarries** near St Keverne from 1890 until the plant was mothballed in 2005.

At one time, the quarry, a key local employer, produced more than 200,000 tons a year of this dense, durable rock, mainly used for roads and coastal defences. Blasted from the quarry face, the stone was pulverised and piled into heaps, graded by size. Until operations ceased, conveyor belts took the crushed rock to a metal jetty where it was loaded into waiting ships at high tide. The narrowness of the local roads

Opposite, top:
The disused Dean Quarry jetty at the northern end of Polcries beach.
RICHARD POWELL

Opposite, bottom:
Dawn breaks over the southern end of Godrevy Cove to the north of Dean Quarry.
RICHARD POWELL

Left: The rusting stone crushing plant at Dean Quarry.
RICHARD POWELL

meant that all the stone was despatched via the sea.

The quarry now is silent, its buildings rusting away, painting a scene of dereliction akin to a decaying inner-city industrial site – not what visitors to the Cornish coast might expect.

Public access to the coast is gained via a winding tarmac road from St Keverne past the farmstead of Trythance. A fieldside path leads down a hillside until the massive expanse of the quarry with its blue-painted steel crushing plant and loading jetty comes starkly into view.

The coast path follows a signposted route through the quarry and on to **Godrevy Cove**, a long, slender beach of pebbles and low-tide sand which can also be reached from the hamlet of Rosenithon.

South from Dean Quarries, the coast path leads to a similar low-water beach, **Polcries**, and then to Lowland Point, an unusually low flat headland now in the care of the National Trust. It is a raised beach, where the original 250ft gabbro cliffs, dating from an epoch when sea levels were much higher than today, are now some distance inland.

About a mile offshore from Dean Quarries can be seen the notorious reef known as the Manacles, which have been the cause of numerous shipwrecks and fatalities over the centuries.

The West of England Quarry at Porthoustock is still in operation.
RICHARD POWELL

Porthkerris Cove as viewed from the bluebell-strewn clifftops in early May. ROBIN JONES

To the north of Manacles Point lies **Porthoustock**, where the extensive cliffside West of England Quarry – still very much in operation producing aggregates – dominates the little fishing village and its pebbly beach.

Shunned by tourists because of the heavy industry aspect, Porthoustock is devoid of commercialisation. It has several splendid traditional cottages, and fishing boats are still winched up on to the shore. There is a "genuine" feel about its day-to-day life sadly no longer apparent in many other places.

Porthkerris Cove, known locally as Kerris, a beach of small, well-smoothed black pebbles lies north of Porthoustock, and can be accessed by car via a series of steep hills and winding high-hedged lanes with stopping places and vantage points offering superb views of Falmouth Bay.

Porthoustock takes part in the traditional Cornish sport of gig racing. RICHARD POWELL

Calm seas in Leggan Cove to the south of Porthoustock. RICHARD POWELL

CHAPTER 20

THE HALCYON HELFORD

Few waterways in Britain can approach the sylvan splendour of the beautiful Helford River, its undisturbed wooded shores and tranquil inlets providing the sharpest dramatic contrast to Cornwall's image of busy holiday beaches and big surfing waves.

The Helford River, not a real river but a tidal creek fed only by a few small streams, escaped large-scale dockyard development because of its proximity to Carrick Roads and the Fal estuary.

The shallow Helford could never match Falmouth's facility as a deepwater port, and while massive ocean-going tankers are regularly seen ploughing through the busy sea lanes in and out of Falmouth Bay, the mouth of the Helford is home only to a flotilla of small motor boats and sailing dinghies, and has thereby retained its time-honoured character.

Opposite: The tiny fishing port of Durgan. Sandy stretches appear at low tide below Durgan and also Grebe beach, Port Saxon and Porthallack to the east. TIM GREEN*

Below: Dusk falls over the Helford River. ANDREW KOSSMAN*

Twisting and often-torturous narrow lanes lead down to the creeks and tiny harbours. There are many spots on both the north and south coasts of the river where it is possible to glean parking space and follow footpaths along the water's edge, but by far the best way to see the Helford is from the water itself; pleasure cruises run daily from Falmouth harbour, often terminating halfway up the river alongside Frenchman's Creek if low tide prevents the head of navigation at **Gweek** being reached.

Flushing, not to be confused with the far larger village on the Fal estuary, has a tiny shingle beach which has some patches of low-tide sand. It is possible to wade across the creek to St Anthony-in-Meneage on ancient stepping stones an hour either side of low tide.

Gillan Creek, on the south bank of the estuary mouth, has been described quite rightly as a miniature version of the Helford.
TIM GREEN*

Above the head of Gillan Creek is the delightful little village of **Manaccan**, with its painted stone cottages and granite church where an immense fig-tree grows out of the walls.

The coastal path leads westwards along a wooded shore and through the private estate of Bosahan to the whitewashed thatched cottages of **Helford**, an old smugglers' village from where a foot ferry to the northern shore has existed since before records began.

To the west lies little **Penarvon Cove** and Pengwedhen Woods, below which is found the little chapel of St Francis, built in 1930 in memory of a yachtsman.

A drive descends to **Tremayne Quay**, built by local lord Sir Richard Vyvian for the sole purpose of receiving Queen Victoria in 1846... only she never came.

The ferry landing point at Helford Passage on the north bank of the river.
TIM GREEN*

A resident of the Cornish Seal Sanctuary at Gweek.
STUART RICHARDS*

A mile inland is the mansion of **Trelowarren**, the seat of the Vyvyans for six centuries. It now has its own inviting little restaurant, a pottery, gift shop, herb nursery and camp site. Trelowarren Gallery holds regular arts and crafts exhibitions.

The uppermost reaches of the Helford spread out into a series of little creeks like a splayed hand, with **Gweek** at the head. Still a centre for boatbuilding, it is the home of the Cornish Seal Sanctuary.

Helford Passage is highly popular as an anchorage and a shingle beach strewn with seaweed is uncovered at low tide.

Two of the very finest nineteenth-century landscaped gardens anywhere in the world are to be found next door to each other – **Trebah** and **Glendurgan**.

Privately-owned Trebah is a spectacular 25-acre garden centred around a ravine where a gushing stream links ponds full of Koi carp and exotic plants by a series of waterfalls. Glendurgan, owned by the National Trust, is the product of the Fox family, who ran the Quaker shipping business in Falmouth in the 1820s and brought exotic species from abroad

Left: Lost in the maze in Glendurgan's gardens.
TIM GREEN*

Below: The stream running through Trebah Gardens ends on a little private beach in Polgwidden Cove, which visitors may use for sunbathing and swimming. It was also one of numerous boarding points for US troops preparing for D-Day.
TIM GREEN*

and grew them here in the warm micro-climate provided by the Gulf Stream and the Helford's sheltered sides.

CHAPTER 21

THE TIP OF THE ROSELAND

"Out on a limb" is the perfect description of the ancient parish of **St Anthony-in-Roseland**, an island all of its own but for 400 yards of hillside.

Not only the Roseland but the whole of the magnificent cliff-backed coast between the sailing haven of St Mawes and the tourist honeypot Mevagissey remains largely uncommer-

cialised, mainly because of the large absence of main roads, while the high-hedged narrow twisting lanes and inclines deter the easily frustrated mass market visitor.

The name Roseland derives from Rhos, meaning headland or peninsula, which it is, just that, a massive promontory bordered by Carrick Roads and Gerrans Bay.

However, St Anthony-in-Roseland is a promontory on a promontory, divided from St Mawes by the half-mile wide

Looking south from Porthmellion Head, the great low-tide stretch of golden sands at Porthbear is one of the Roseland's many hidden treasures. CHRISTINE MOON

estuary of the Percuil River, and is attached to the mainland only by the slender neck of land between **Towan beach** and **Froe Creek** upon which Porth Farm stands. The old name for the parish of St Anthony was Rhos Innis – island of Roseland.

The lane south from Portscatho and its twin village Gerrans always seems to take forever, yet it is less than 4 miles to St Anthony's Head.

Tiny **Froe** on Froe Creek was once a bustling little port in its own right, with small boats sailing up the Percuil River to discharge cargoes of coal until early in the twentieth century. Now it remains silent, the woods above Porth Creek being the nesting place for herons.

Seaward of Froe lies a sizeable National Trust car park serving the large dune-backed and totally unspoiled **Towan beach** 200 yards away.

Opposite, top: Great Molunan beach lies to the immediate north of St Anthony Head lighthouse. IAN SWITHINBANK*

Opposite, bottom: Towan beach is owned by the National Trust and lies to the north of Killigeran Head. IAN SWITHINBANK*

Below: This enticing beach with its turquoise Mediterranean waters lies blow the hamlet of Treloan to the south of Portscatho. TIM GREEN*

The lighthouse at
Anthony Head has a
range of 14 miles.
TRINITY HOUSE

The lane ascends sharply from Porth Farm and soon the lonely hamlet of Bohortha is reached. A steep zigzag path accesses secluded **Porthbeor beach**, a long expanse of low tide sand and rocks where swimming is dangerous.

St Anthony Head has the ruins of a Victorian gun battery which was also later modified and saw service in both world wars.

A three-minute walk leads to the now-automated **St Anthony lighthouse** which was built to improve safety near the dreaded Manacles.

None of the excellent walks along the shores of the **Percuil River** and its tributaries are more delightful than the stretch from **Place** which winds its way eastwards to Porth Farm a mile and a half away. An historic ferry service between Place and St Mawes was reinstated in 1991.

View of the Percuil River from Place House at St Anthony-in-Roseland. TIM GREEN*

CHAPTER 22

VERYAN BAY AND THE DEADLY DODMAN

Narrow, single track lanes with traditional Cornish high hedges made from earthen banks turn and twist endlessly and seemingly aimlessly under thick canopies of leafy boughs.

When the end of each winding valley is finally reached by the frustrated motorist, little pearls of half-forgotten fishing harbours and idyllic grey-sand sand coves lie in wait.

The rural triangle between St Mawes, Tregony and Mevagissey is markedly different from anywhere else in Cornwall; the lack of main or even straight roads and the total absence of railways has preserved its unique rustic timelessness.

Summer sees the very limited available car parking spaces at the tiny beaches soon fill up. However, rarely is there the lack of breathing space you find elsewhere in August.

The 10-mile coastal stretch between **Portloe** and Portmellon is a treasure. The slate cottages of Portloe, in so many ways a perfect 'typical' Cornish fishing village, are huddled together between the cliffs of the rocky inlet in which it is nestled.

At Portloe, a handful of fisherman still draw their small boats up on the little stone slipway, and it still has its own Harbour Commission and harbourmasters despite its Liliputian size!

The Ship Inn has for decades been renowned for the locally-caught crab served in sumptuous sandwiches and salads. The only hotel is the Lugger, a seventeenth-century inn built above the slipway near the old pilchard cellars; a former landlord, Black Dunstan, was hanged for smuggling.

Two roads lead out of Portloe, the west route leading to **Veryan**, famous for its curious round houses, two miles away. Five of these quaint whitewashed cottages, each with a stone cross on the rooftop, were built in the nineteenth century in a fashion supposedly designed to keep the devil out.

The east road out of Portloe twists its way uphill for half a mile before descending to the epitome of south Cornwall's

Opposite, top:
The slipway at Portloe is still part of a working harbour.
EDWARD WEBB*

Opposite, bottom:
A pair of the famous Veryan round houses.
ROBIN JONES

pocket-sized harbours and ancient fishing coves, the enchanting little hamlets of **East** and **West Portholland**.

The next beach, **Porthluney Cove**, lies a mile eastwards by the cliff path, but can also be accessed by winding roads, and offers basic facilities and safe bathing.

Behind the beach, fairytale **Caerhays Castle** is a mock Gothic fortress built in 1808.

Above: Caerhays Castle at Porthluney Cove and its gardens are open to the public. ROBIN JONES

Below left: Some of the exquisite blooms to be seen in the grounds of Caerhays Castle where spring comes early. STEPHEN KELLY

Opposite, top: Sandy Porthluney Cove lies below the castle. ROBIN JONES

Opposite, bottom: A concrete sea wall defends tiny East Portholland from storm surges. ROBIN JONES

The most delightful cove of all in Veryan Bay is tiny **Hemmick Beach**, a mile and a half east of Porthluney by inland road or a coastal path which opens up much inspiring cliff scenery despite the presence of brambles in places. A narrow lane leads down to the beach from the hamlet of Boswinger.

Sailors always had just cause to fear the **Dodman**, a

shadowy treacherous promontory which juts into the English Channel like a dark, demonic, sleeping dragon.

A massive granite cross on the summit of this 373ft-high headland was erected by the vicar of nearby St Michael Caerhays in 1896 as a daylight guide for seafarers.

The Iron Age cliff castle on the summit is one of the biggest and best preserved in Cornwall.

Above: The huge granite cross on Dodman Point was erected by a local vicar in a bid to save lives. DAVE DUMMETT www.davedummett photography.co.uk

Left: Hemmick's sands are uncovered by the ebbing tide; bathing is good and there are many rocky ledges ideal for picnics. ROBIN JONES

CHAPTER 23
AROUND GORRAN HAVEN

From the Dodman, the flat narrow lane from Penare eastwards to **Gorran Haven** known as the Gruda is a delight to drive along; unfenced on the seaward side, it offers splendid sweeping channel views.

A car park at Lamledra Farm gives access both to Maenease Point, which shelters the old fishing village of Gorran Haven to the north, and the splendid Vault or **Bow beach** directly below the bracken and heather-covered cliffsides.

A safe path leads down to this long beach of gritty sand, which by virtue of its isolation has been used as an unofficial nudist beach in recent times.

Vault or Bow beach on the eastern side of the Dodman. KAREN WITHAK

The small harbour of Gorran Haven has largely escaped the commercialisation of neighbouring Mevagissey.
STEVE PARKER

Although there is some modern bungalow development on its outskirts, Gorran Haven has also escaped mass commercialisation.

A stone breakwater protects the village's little sandy beach. The quay was built in 1885 and replaced six previous attempts at harbours, all of which were smashed to rubble by storms. A little chapel dedicated to St Just is intriguingly perched amongst the fishermen's cottages right above the beach.

North of Gorran Haven lies sandy Great Perhaver beach, accessible only by boat or swimming round rocks from Little Perhaver at low tide.
JONATHAN CHARLES

The coastal path leads on to Great Perhaver beach, which is almost a carbon copy of Vault beach.

Northwards along unspoilt cliff tops and passing more prehistoric earthworks is Turbot Point which overlooks stony

Gulls nest in the
red cliffs at Great
Perhaver beach.
JONATHAN CHARLES

Colona beach. Here, legend states, local aristocrat Sir Henry Trenowth of Bodrugan leapt from the cliffs on his horse after being chased by his old enemy, Sir Richard Edgcumbe of Cotehele, who he had victimised under Richard III, and whose fortunes had changed following Henry VII's victory in the Wars of the Roses. The story says that Trenowth escaped in a waiting boat to France.

Unlike Gorran Haven, the bigger fishing port of Mevagissey succumbed to the mass tourist market early on, and it shows.

However, to the north of Mevagissey there is the promontory of Black Head, with a tiny sand and pebble cove below Hallane Mill where solitude is all but guaranteed.

The small sand and
pebble Hallane Cove.
ALI PACKHAM

CHAPTER 24

THE DREAMSCAPE OF DAPHNE DU MAURIER

Daphne du Maurier, the Queen of Cornish romance chanced upon Menabilly in the 1930s, turning it into a fairytale kingdom entirely of her own but one which forever enchanted the rest of the world.

A mysterious mansion still hidden in landscaped parkland and deep woods away from the gaze of passers-by; a navigation mark which all but resembles a stick of red-and-white striped candy; lonely sandy coves with a house right on the shore and a miniature fishing harbour reached down a woody glen...for Daphne du Maurier, these are certainly the stuff that dreams were made of.

Daphne discovered the house when holidaying with her family at Fowey in the thirties. It was the ancestral seat of the Rashleigh family, for centuries the major landowners in the area, but had become neglected and the front was largely obscured by unchecked ivy. Enchanted by the Menabilly estate, Daphne obtained permission to wander over the land.

Menabilly largely inspired her phenomenally-successful international bestseller Rebecca, published in 1938, and the opening lines recalled that bramble-choked driveway:

"Last night I dreamt I went to Manderley again. It seemed to me I stood by the iron gate leading to the drive..."

The boathouse on the shore of **Polridmouth** (Pridmouth) beach was the model for the cottage where Rebecca entertained her guests and where she was supposedly murdered.

Profits from Daphne's writing allowed her to return to Menabilly during World War Two and lease the rundown house she alone adored, and the surrounding landscape inspired many of her subsequent works.

The Queen, Prince Philip and other members of the Royal Family were guests of Daphne and her husband at Menabilly. However, she was heartbroken when her Rashleigh landlords demanded to move back into the house. In 1967, Daphne, by then a widow, moved "next door" to fourteenth-century Kilmarth, a dower house to Menabilly, which overlooks Par Sands.

Opposite, top: Seaweed-strewn Polridmouth beach at low tide. ROBIN JONES

Opposite, bottom: Polridmouth Cottage, in fiction Rebecca's private haunt, is part of an old water-mill belonging to the Rashleigh estate. The freshwater ornamental lake was created in the 1930s by damming up the small stream which once turned the water wheel and in World War Two floodlights were fixed around it to create an illusion of Fowey, a port used by the Allies for the D-Day landings, to confuse enemy aircraft. ROBIN JONES

Above: The red-and white 84ft daymark, striped like a square barbershop pole which stands half a mile to the east on top of 240-feet high Gribbin Head, built in 1832 by Trinity House as a marker to help lost sailors tell the difference between the shallows of St Austell Bay and the safe entrance to Falmouth harbour.
ROBIN JONES

Right: The inaccessible sandy cove of Platt as seen from Gribbin Head.
ROBIN JONES

Two public car parks serve this stretch of coast – the National Trust one at Coombe, reached via the Lankelly Farm end of Fowey, or the more immediate one at Menabilly Barton farm, accessed by a sharp turn off the A3082 at the top of the hill overlooking Par. From both, there is a half a mile walk along well-marked footpaths to the coast.

The twin grey-sand beaches of Polridmouth are sheltered from south-westerly winds by Gribbin Head and its stripy daymark, a visual aid to passing ships. In the rocks between the coves lies an oblong hole which fills with seawater at high tide, with steps leading into it; this was a bathtub cut for the Rashleighs.

The coastal path to the west leads above Platt, a large inaccessible sandy expanse, to Little Gribbin and then northwards to the little pocket harbour of **Polkerris** a mile to the north. Polkerris can also be reached by car, turning off the Menabilly road just before the little Tregaminion wayside chapel.

The quay, built by the Rashleighs in 1700, protects a small sandy low-tide beach, where deckchairs can be hired.

Daphne du Maurier, a Dame Commander of the Order of the British Empire, became increasingly reclusive in her latter years, and died in her sleep on 19 April 1989, at the age of 81.

Polkerris was a major port for landing pilchards and boasted Cornwall's biggest seine house, or 'pilchard palace' where the fish were processed for oil. ROBIN JONES

The Menabilly estate's little Tregaminion chapel, built by William Rashleigh in 1816. ROBIN JONES

CHAPTER 25

DONKEY TRACKS TO DISTANT COVES

Sizeable Lansallos
Cove at low tide.
BEN CHAPMAN.

Staying power and bags of energy are definitely needed if you want to explore the finest hidden beaches and coves in south-east Cornwall.

It is so easy to be drawn down inviting cliff and valley paths trimmed with masses of bluebells and primroses in spring...forgetting the fact you have to climb nearly 400ft back to the top again.

The mere thought of having to cart all that beach clobber up the hill again in the blistering August heat deters many holidaymakers from discovering the superb niches below the cliffs between Polruan and Polperro.

A narrow but delightfully straight lane leads off the B3359 south of Lanreath and leads to **Lansallos** village.

Lansallos appears to have originated around a medieval monastery, possibly founded by the obscure St Salwys, while little more is known about St Ildierna, to who the prominent fourteenth-century church is dedicated.

The path to the beach leads along the drive to the right of the church gate. The sheltered tree-lined path has Redd Water, a babbling brook, gushing along at the side.

Descending sharply towards the cove, the stream cascades

to the shore via a waterfall. The final few yards of the path to the beach run through an ancient gully hewn through the cliffside, once used by farmers taking donkey cartloads of sand and seaweed for fertiliser.

The enchanting little semi-circular grey-sand cove is backed by slate cliffs with alternating pink and green streaks.

A short walk up the cliffs on the eastern side of the beach will take the very agile to the next sandy inlet, Parson's Cove, reached by carefully inching your way down its eastern side. Palace Cove lies a third of a mile westwards, and beyond there is Sandingway, also accessed by a public footpath from a National Trust car park at Frogmore Farm a third of a mile to the north.

Spectacular **Lantic Bay** is reached by a gently-sloping path along the grassy contours of the rounded cliffside to a point where a sharper and near-vertical climb down to Great Lantic Beach can be undertaken.

Those who accept the big slog back up are rewarded by the stunning beauty of Great Lantic Beach and its sister, Little Lantic Beach, both backed by yellow gorse-matted cliffsides.

Lansallos church of St Ildierna. A tombstone near the gate records the death of "John Perry, Mariner", a smuggler "kill'd by a cannon ball" in 1779 when just 24: the inscription reads: "I by a shot which rapid flew was instantly struck dead, Lord pardon the offender who my precious blood did shed." ROBIN JONES

Lantic Bay, well worth the Herculean effort to climb back up. ROBIN JONES

CHAPTER 26
THEY BOUGHT AN ISLAND

Many people often daydream about throwing it all in and setting up home on a secluded island. Very few, however, turn such dreams into reality.

Main: Looe Island, as seen from Hannafore Point.
ROBIN JONES

Inset: Barry the bull seal near the island jetty.
CLAIRE LEWIS

Among their number can be counted sisters Babs and Evelyn Atkins, who in 1965 bought 22½-acre **St George's** or **Looe Island**, off Hannafore Point.

The island, 150ft high at its summit, was like St Michael's Mount settled by Benedictine monks, who in 1139 built a chapel dedicated to the same saint. Channel 4's *Time Team* excavated the site in 2008 and a hoard of Roman coins was found.

Silver washed
fritillary on a teasel
on Looe Island.
CLAIRE LEWIS

The island later passed into the ownership of Glastonbury Abbey, which may have acquired it to profit from the medieval "holiday traffic", with pilgrims journeying to sites associated with St Michael.

When Henry VIII dissolved the monasteries, the island passed to the Crown.

After buying the island, Evelyn worked as a teacher in Looe and at first came just for the weekends, but Babs lived there permanently. There was no telephone, and the only means of communicating with the shore was by flag or hand signal.

Nevertheless, the winters were by and large exceptionally mild, with daffodils blooming as early as December.

Evelyn wrote two books about their life on the island, *We Bought An Island* and its sequel *Tales From Our Cornish Island*.

Evelyn died in 1997 at the age of 87, but Babs continued to live on the island until her death in 2004 aged 86. She left the island to the Cornwall Wildlife Trust which has maintained it as a nature reserve.

Landing charges collected from summer day visitors, who take boat trips from Looe, are used to maintain the island's basic facilities and do as much as possible to keep it in the way that nature intended.

The island has two beaches which offer safe bathing, a natural rock swimming pool, caves and walks through the woodland. A trail takes visitors to the main points of interest including the chapel.

There are several different natural habitats including woodland, maritime grassland, sand, shingle and rocky reefs, and seals can be spotted swimming in the waters around its rocky coves.

Opposite, top:
Visitors disembarking
from the island boat,
the *Islander*.
CLAIRE LEWIS

Opposite, bottom:
Looe Island House
and cliffs. JON ROSS

135

CHAPTER 27
CORNWALL'S FORGOTTEN CORNER

We now end our journey with a whole section of Cornwall, towns and all, which have literally been bypassed by the mass tourist market.

The area west of Crafthole and Portwrinkle, bounded by the Lynher River on one side, the Tamar on the other and the English Channel on the third has come to be known as Cornwall's "forgotten corner", and includes the Rame peninsula, which forms a south-eastern 'dog leg' of the duchy.

The Great Western Railway ran straight past it, and so do most visitors who head over the Tamar on the A38 road bridge en route to Newquay, St Ives and other popular destinations much further into Cornwall.

Beginning in the west at the small fishing village of **Portwrinkle**, despite much modern bungalow development around it, its historic heart with its old fishermen's cottages remains unspoilt.

The old quay pier was smashed by the raging sea during a storm in 1882. The remains of the old harbour wall can still be seen, with a newer breakwater built inside it.

East of Portwrinkle lies a spectacular 4-mile stretch of sand, one of Cornwall's longest and perhaps most beautiful beaches. However, deceptive **Whitsand Bay** has been the death of many a swimmer over the years because of a tidal race and strong undercurrents caused by underwater gullies.

The monstrous disused limestone military fort above the cliffs at Tregantle is the westernmost point in a defensive ring constructed around Plymouth in the 1860s under the direction of Lord Palmerston in response to fears about the French emperor Napoleon III's intentions.

Turning at right angles off the B3247 is a former military road opened to the public in 1930. This coastal road hugs the clifftops to Freathy, Withnoe and beyond to Rame.

Before Freathy is reached, halfway down the steep cliff path to the beach at **Sharrow Point**, below the lookout station, is a man-made grotto which has poetry written on the roof! Known as Lugger's Cave after its creator, James Lugger, a Naval officer

Opposite, top:
The inner core of present-day Portwrinkle is surprisingly untarnished by tourism. Willow or "withy" is still grown locally for making crab pots.
ROBIN JONES

Opposite, bottom:
Whitsand Bay at high tide becomes a string of coves.
ROBIN JONES

Tregantle is the
only one of the
Palmerston forts
around Plymouth
still used by the
Army as a firing
range.
PHILIP HALLING*

invalided through gout after the American War of Independence, this 7-feet-high chamber penetrates about 15ft into the cliffs. He carved his own verse as decoration on the walls of his cave, and fitted a stone bench for visitors.

Access to the sands can be gained via a steep path from **Freathy**, a chalet village. Tregonhawke has a car park for another access path, while an old sand track at Wiggle Cliff a mile to the east also provides a reasonable route down.

The sandy sweep of the bay ends in a series of rocky beds before sheltered Polhawn Cove, the safest of all the coves and beaches at Whitsand. Polhawn Fort, another of the Palmerston fortifications, is now a hotel.

The 'almost-island' of **Rame Head** is linked to the 'mainland' by a neck of land 200 yards wide, with sheer cliffs on

Grotto beach at Sharrow Point as seen from the lookout point halfway down the access path.
ROBIN JONES

139

Rame Head viewed
from the west.
ROBIN JONES

either side; a perfect site for another Iron Age cliff castle.

On the 300ft-high summit stands a thirteenth-century chapel dedicated yet again to St Michael, where beacon fires have been lit there in times of crisis, such as the arrival of the Spanish Armada on 20 July 1588.

Cawsand beach at
the crack of dawn.
ROBIN JONES

Below the Penlee Point signal station a path leads to a tiny sandy cove. First you must pass Adelaide Chapel, one of

several follies built on the Mount Edgcumbe estate.

The now-linked twin villages of **Cawsand** and **Kingsand** are among the finest examples of traditional and largely unspoiled Cornish fishing ports.

Cornish? Until 1841, the border with Devon passed between the two villages leaving Maker and Mount Edgcumbe in that county; a house in Garrett Street opposite the Halfway House Inn aptly named Devon Corn proudly displays the old boundary mark on its front wall to this day. This anomaly dates back to the Saxon conquest of the Celtic kingdom of Dumnonii when the invaders seized control of the strategic heights overlooking the Tamar.

Full of quaint picture-postcard painted cottages in narrow, winding streets, these villages have escaped the blight of boarding house development and trashy souvenir shops.

Cawsand was a major centre for smuggling in the seventeenth century because its sheltered deepwater position commanding vantage points allowed ample warning of the Revenue men, and John Carter, the King of Prussia, had connections here.

Kingsand village: when returned to Cornwall in 1844, it had been part of Devon for a millennium!
ROBIN JONES

The real heyday of both Cawsand and Kingsand came when the Channel Fleet made use of the deepwater anchorage here towards the close of the eighteenth century, making the villages safe from attack.

Both villages have small sand and shingle beaches which are safe for bathing, and boats can be hired.

To the north, Tudor **Mount Edgcumbe House**, burned out by an incendiary bomb dropped during the blitz of 1941, is now in public ownership and has been restored with eighteenth century decor. It is now the centre of a massive country park, open to everyone all the year round free of charge.

In 1695, the traveller Celia Fiennes described the **Cremyll** to Stonehouse ferry, as a "hazardous passage by reason of three tides meeting" which lasted an hour.

Today's far safer ferry brings droves of summer visitors across the Hamoaze, the estuary of the Tamar.

If you have progressed this far, you might like to end our journey around the secrets of the Cornish coast with a cool

The imposing front of Mount Edgcumbe House, the former seat of the Earls of Mount Edgcumbe. DENNA JONES*

The regular foot ferry from Cremyll to Stonehouse in Devon. DENNA JONES*

pint in the fifteenth-century Edgcumbe Arms overlooking the water at the end of the delectable duchy.

A ruin that is not a ruin as it was deliberately built as such: the folly in Mount Edgcumbe Country Park overlooking Plymouth Sound. Dating from 1747, it replaced an obelisk which had stood on the site. IAN SWITHINBANK*

INDEX